Hospital Treatment and Care

1853027448

Living with Serious Mental Illness series

Getting Into the System
Living with Serious Mental Illness
Gwen Howe
ISBN 1 85302 457 0
Living with Serious Mental Illness 1

Mental Health Assessments
Gwen Howe
ISBN 1 85302 458 9
Living with Serious Mental Illness 2

of related interest

Working with Schizophrenia
A Needs Based Approach
Gwen Howe
ISBN 1 85302 242 X

Psychosis
Understanding and Treatment
Edited by Jane Ellwood
ISBN 1 85302 265 9

Managing Manic Depressive Disorders
Edited by Ved Varma
ISBN 1 85302 347 7

LIVING WITH SERIOUS MENTAL ILLNESS 3

Hospital Treatment and Care

Gwen Howe

Jessica Kingsley Publishers
London and Philadelphia

This edition first published in the United Kingdom in 1999 by
Jessica Kingsley Publishers Ltd,
116 Pentonville Road,
London N1 9JB,
England
and
325 Chestnut Street,
Philadelphia, PA 19106, USA.

www.jkp.com

Copyright © 1999 Gwen Howe

ISBN 1 85302 744 8

Library of Congress Cataloging in Publication Data
A CIP catalog record for this book is available from the Library of Congress

British Library Cataloguing in Publication Data
A CIP catalogue record for this book is available from the British Library

Printed and Bound in Great Britain by
Athenaeum Press, Gateshead, Tyne and Wear

Contents

This book is dedicated to Rachel Shadbolt, Occupational Therapist, in recognition of her untiring efforts on behalf of those sufferers who have 'slipped through the net' or have to cope with a particularly severe illness.

A note on royalties

Forty per cent of any royalties from this book will be shared between the Manic Depression Fellowship and a local group of the National Schizophrenia Fellowship.

Preface

At a time when those who work with serious mental illness are being encouraged to listen more keenly to sufferers and carers, the *Living with Serious Mental Illness* series provides an impressive opportunity for the consumer to speak and to be heard.

About the series

Each of the books in this series focuses on a different aspect of the mental health services, with the aim of contributing to a better understanding of the experiences and needs of those having to rely on the present system. A group of carers and sufferers have met together to select case studies known to them and to analyse and discuss these. They have brought with them their own individual experiences and expertise to highlight some of the problems which can make it difficult to obtain appropriate help at the right time. By doing this, they believe that this series will enable students to appreciate at an early stage the crucial issues which influence whether or not a sufferer survives to enjoy a reasonable quality of life, and provide an opportunity for professionals to take a fresh look at and perhaps reconsider their own practice in the light of the experiences discussed.

As the author, I am writing this series with, and on behalf of, an Essex-based pressure group of consumers. Its name – the LEAP group – stands for Living with the Experience of Acute Psychosis.

About the LEAP group

This group was formed in 1995, with twelve members. Of these, five have personal experience of a psychotic illness such as manic depression (MD) or schizophrenia. The others are close relatives of a sufferer although one of them has also suffered with a depressive illness himself. The only change which has taken place in the membership of the group since the beginning of the series is that one carer has dropped out during the writing of this third book, *Hospital Treatment and Care*.

More about the group's members

As a matter of interest, members of the group, whose ages range from 34 to 68 years, come from very diverse backgrounds and, to a quite remarkable extent, they represent virtually the whole gamut of income levels throughout our society. Four of the group have honours degrees to their credit and one has a recent masters degree. All have experience of working, as professionals or volunteers, with the seriously mentally ill. All have been involved in speaking in public about their experiences or taking part in professionals' training programmes. All have had their own real and time-consuming problems in the past – some continue to have them – and yet they find time to continue to campaign for a better deal for everyone who has to find ways of coping with a serious mental illness. Of the five group members with personal experience of serious mental illness, one is retired but still active in the community, one is a voluntary worker, one is a very busy young mother and two have responsible full-time jobs.

The role of the group

In each book, the LEAP group is responsible for providing the input which appears under the headings *GROUP'S ANALYSIS OF CASE STUDY* and *THE WIDER PERSPECTIVE* and this is collated in the following ways:

1. by members completing questionnaires sent out with each draft case study, while adding as much comment and information as they feel to be relevant.

2. from discussion at group meetings dedicated to individual case studies.

3. from several members in turn adding their comments to completed case studies.

In addition, the contract between members of the group and myself allows the group's Chair, who has personal experience of a serious mental illness, to read and edit each chapter and a further member to read and edit the complete book prior to its going to the publisher. It also allows for any member of the group to read and comment on any chapter at any time.

The structure of each book

Each book has a similar format. The first and last chapters take the form of an **introduction** and a **summing up** by myself. The intervening chapters focus on separate case studies, each dealing with one aspect of one individual's experience of 'the system'. The last of these chapters is devoted to several case studies to broaden the scope of the experience covered in each book. In the present book there is an added feature – in order to better appreciate the consumer's experience of hospital care, Chapter 7 looks at a list of needs which too often seem to be overlooked when sufferers are in hospital.

The structure of each of the chapters focusing on a case study

These chapters are made up of a **case study** and a short **comment** which includes a pause for thought and an opportunity to undertake an informal exercise. This is followed by the **group's analysis of the case study** and its discussion of **the wider perspective**. The chapter ends with a short **summing up**, relevant **information** and an **exercise**.

Under the heading **comment**, it has been assumed that readers may be interested in critically examining what is happening in individual case studies, perhaps with the help of an informal exercise, before going on to read the LEAP group's findings. This could be achieved within a group training context or, equally well, by working on one's own and making appropriate notes before proceeding with the rest of the chapter.

Under the heading **information**, references and extra information are provided which tie up with matters highlighted in case studies, the LEAP group's analysis and their further discussion. There may be some repetition under this heading to save the need for cross referencing and so ensure that each chapter is complete in itself for training purposes.

Under the heading **exercise**, a project is proposed which is suitable for use in a group training context or as a formal piece of written work.

Case studies

The subject of each case study may be a member of the LEAP group, or a relative, friend or acquaintance of a member. It is important that group members come from several different geographical areas and some of them are also involved nationally or regionally in the voluntary sector. Thus case studies are drawn from a nationwide sample. Because of this diverse experience within the group, we are assured that consumers can have remarkably similar experiences throughout England and Wales. However, when it comes to the particular subject of this book, we are aware that there can be a dramatic difference between life on the wards of provincial hospitals in the 1990s and those seemingly struggling against all the odds in inner-cities. Particular reference has been made to this in Chapter 1. On a happier note, we are very pleased to point out that this third book in the series is enriched by the personal testimonies of several of the sufferers featured in its case studies. Having said that, please do note that names and other details which are irrelevant to the basic facts of each case have been changed to protect the identity of sufferers (whether or not they are happy to 'go public'), their families and, most important, the service providers involved.

What's in a name?

As I have mentioned in introductions to my previous books, it is a problem for an author to know how best to refer to individuals who have to cope with the condition which is the subject of their book and also how to refer to those most involved with these individuals. For some, this is an important issue but it is also one on which there is little agreement. Until this situation resolves itself, I hope readers will continue to bear with me while I use the terms 'sufferers' and 'carers' in the interests of expediency and a readable writing style.

Members of the LEAP group have had similar difficulties deciding what to call themselves for the purposes of this series. Several of those who might in other circumstances be labelled with the fashionable word 'user' were adamantly against this and, in the context of their involvement in this series, there was little enthusiasm for the word 'sufferer' either. They eventually settled for the word 'survivor', acknowledging that lots of individuals, like themselves, are fortunate enough to find ways of largely coping with, and surviving, a serious mental illness.

Similarly, those members of the group who are relatives of individuals having to cope with a serious mental illness were not too sure about the word 'carer' as they not only feel that the word is abused by the system, they also find it rather patronizing to refer to themselves as carers. In the event, and like others before them, they nevertheless opted for the term 'carer' for the sake of convenience and clarity, with nothing better coming to mind.

A message for professionals working with serious mental illness

The LEAP group members have asked me to point out that as they are campaigning for better services for everyone who has to cope with a psychotic illness, it is essential that they highlight where things go wrong. They would not wish this in any way to detract from the splendid work of some caring and dedicated professionals out there whose untiring efforts enable sufferers to get on successfully with their lives. Members suspect that these professionals are the same ones who will be most interested in reading a series like this although it does not allow for more than a passing comment on their invaluable contribution to a deserving, but largely neglected, cause. The group would like to take this opportunity of saying a special 'thank you' on behalf of those sufferers who have received the sort of treatment and care which has freed them to get on with the rest of their lives despite having to cope with a serious mental illness.

Gwen Howe,
April 1999

CHAPTER 1

Hospital treatment and care
An introduction

Serious mental illness is the name we give to conditions such as manic depression (MD) and schizophrenia. We use the word 'serious' (although sufferers can be relatively well much of the time) because at times of breakdown they can lose touch with reality. This is called a psychotic episode.

Psychosis is dangerous because sufferers are no longer able to understand what is happening around them and, in particular, have little or no awareness that they are ill and in need of help. At this point, often terrified and paranoid, it is vital that they are protected from themselves and from any immediate dangers. They also need protecting from the ravages of an untreated psychosis as this can inflict irreversible damage to their health and, at worst, lead into an intractable chronic illness. The flip-side of this is that psychosis is eminently treatable and during the past two decades there has been mounting evidence to support the reasonable assumption that the earlier the appropriate treatment is offered the better the prognosis will be (1). However, as we have observed before in this series, prompt help is the exception rather than the rule, both at the time of a first episode and also at the time of relapse. This means that once deterioration takes place sufferers, more often than not, have to endure long delays until they are eventually admitted to an acute psychiatric ward during the, by then, inevitable crisis. This book is all about what happens from this point onwards.

A time of low morale?

During the last few years of the twentieth century morale among mental health professionals working in hospitals seems to have reached an all-time low. Not only have most of the old mental hospitals closed during the last two decades, but those which remain partly open are run down and bereft of their old bustling communities. It is not surprising that hospital nurses feel that they are working in a vacuum. Their patients are more often than not deprived of the sort of activities which used to be provided by occupational therapy departments and many other features which used to be a part of the everyday life of these hospitals. New psychiatric units – some of which are located many floors up within modern general hospitals – may be well resourced but they lack some of the amenities which were so highly valued by patients, not least the sanctuary of the serene and spacious grounds which were the legacy of the Victorian asylums. While most of us may not grieve for these big old institutions, there remains little doubt that the baby has been thrown out with the bath water and that we have lost some of the more positive features of life in the old hospitals.

Hospitals in inner-cities

Continuing reports testify that inner-city hospitals are crowded to crisis point and ward teams working within them are constantly having to concern themselves with freeing beds still needed by their patients for others waiting outside whose plight is even more urgent. It is not surprising therefore that doctors and nurses trying to cope in these conditions are under constant pressure and are not likely to gain much job satisfaction when much of the time they can only offer this 'too little too late' service for their patients. Meanwhile, we are told that women report violence, even rape, within some of these hospitals and doctors are, in some cases, reluctant to admit female patients even though they may urgently need treatment and care. On a more positive note, the current Labour government has listened to women's pleas for more security in hospitals and in particular for a return to segregated accommodation for the sexes within psychiatric units and wards and this is gradually becoming the norm again for the first time since the 1950s.

A possibly unrepresentative sample?

I mention the current concerns about inner-city hospitals because they have not been covered in *Hospital Treatment and Care*. The case studies featured in the first two books of this series are representative of the sort of experiences found in many parts of England and Wales, whereas those featured in this book do not include any which describe life in these inner-city hospitals at the end of the 1990s. While it is important to point this out, neither I nor the members of the LEAP group feel that this fact in any way detracts from the testimonies of individuals who have been admitted to hospitals with less hazardous and crowded situations. In support of this, we find that recent research reveals that there tends to be more similarities than differences in the complaints made by patients in acute psychiatric wards in both provincial and city hospitals in various parts of England and Wales (2).

The very real problems some of the patients discuss in this book would seem to reinforce a growing feeling that all is not right with psychiatric hospital treatment and care. Indeed, a recent survey carried out by the National Schizophrenia Fellowship (3) found that there was a 'dislike and fear of hospital among service users, often based on intensely distressing personal experience' and The Sainsbury Centre for Mental Health's survey *Acute Problems* (mentioned in (2)), which involved 215 patients in nine acute psychiatric wards across the country, concluded that 'inpatient care is unpopular'. What then is going wrong?

Problem areas?

The Sainsbury Centre for Mental Health's survey concludes that the core problems seem to be that:

- there are no clear goals for acute care
- the setting is neither pleasant nor therapeutic
- staff are not delivering targeted programmes to improve users' health or social functioning, based on individual needs
- acute care is not seen as part of a system of mental health care – connections with community services are poor.

The latter observation may partly account for the fact that discharge was often found to be unplanned with inadequate involvement of community staff, patients and carers. In fact, the survey found that only 34 per cent of patients had a discharge planning meeting, most patients had no idea that they were to be discharged until a few days before they left, and had little involvement in discussions about their future. Almost half of all patients in the survey said that they had not received enough information about their illness and the possible treatments. Most patients were bored during their stay and few if any were involved in planned programmes of social activity, with 40 per cent of all patients undertaking no social or recreational activity.

Bearing in mind these findings about lack of information and stimulation, perhaps we should not be too surprised at a finding reported in a piece of research carried out by The Sainsbury Centre for Mental Health, in collaboration with the Mental Health Act Commission (4); at the time when Commissioners arrived on unannounced visits to acute psychiatric wards throughout England and Wales one morning in 1996, they found there was no nurse involvement with patients on one-quarter of all the wards.

As we shall see, the findings reported in *Hospital Treatment and Care* very much endorse those quoted above. More worrying perhaps, the LEAP group's work has highlighted several instances of a dramatic variation in approach to treatment and care towards the same illness in any one patient at any one time. In short, there seems to have been no standardization of approach to, or care and treatment for, serious mental illness during the past two decades.

We have, of course, come across happy experiences as well as near-disastrous ones while working on this book and these are also recorded here. They have, however, tended to add to our confusion as the three individuals featured in these particular case studies have actually also been subjected to what may well be described as disturbingly negative experiences.

Another way forward?

As members of the LEAP group have to cope with a serious mental illness either personally or as the loved one of a sufferer, they have a vested interest in campaigning for better services. It is fortunate that, despite having to cope with the sort of problems that this type of illness presents, they have found time to look very carefully at the experiences cited in the case studies here and to reconsider – in Chapter 7 – their own experiences and those of their families and friends. In doing this, they have once again, as with the previous books in this series, come up with recommendations which they feel might help to standardize the quality of care and treatment provided and at the same time better serve all of those trying to survive a serious mental illness without suffering unnecessary damage along the way.

INFORMATION

The following pieces of information are relevant to points brought up during the introduction which have been highlighted in the text:

(1) A need for early intervention

Although isolated voices have been heard throughout most of this century protesting that delays in treating psychosis can be permanently damaging to the individual's mental health, it is only during the past two decades that the cry has been taken up by many of those whose work with this type of illness is already highly respected. It is not surprising that the resultant research is now beginning to back up the logical viewpoint that this type of illness is no different to any other, in that early intervention is paramount. What is surprising is that, up to the time of writing, there has been no sign of the system changing to meet the urgent need to prevent this unnecessary damage and further suffering. For some of the relevant studies and access to others, see the following:

(a) A large extended study of first episodes of schizophrenia revealed that the most important determinant of relapse was the duration of illness prior to starting neuroleptic medication (Crow, T.J. *et al.* (1986) 'The Northwick Park study of first episodes of schizophrenia, part II: A randomized controlled trial of prophylactic neuroleptic treatment.' *British Journal of Psychiatry 148*, 120–127).

(b) Not long after Crow (1986) was published, workers conducting a follow-up study of schizophrenia across North America, claimed that it may take only one year of active illness for deterioration or a 'threshold of chronicity' to be reached (McGlashan, T.H. (1988) 'A selective review of recent North American long-term follow-up studies of schizophrenia.' *Schizophrenia Bulletin 14*, 4, 515–542).

(c) A Tokyo University study showed that patients who had had symptoms longer than 1 year before entering treatment were more likely to relapse than patients who were treated within the year (Anzai, N. *et al.* (1988) 'Early neuroleptic medication within one year after onset can reduce risk of later relapses in schizophrenic patients.' *Annual Report Pharmacopsychiatric Research Foundation 19*, 258–265).

(d) Richard Jed Wyatt concluded, in his comprehensive overview of the use of neuroleptic medication and the natural course of schizophrenia, that 'some patients are left with a damaging residual effect if a psychosis is allowed to proceed unmitigated. While psychosis is undoubtedly demoralising and stigmatising, it may also be biologically toxic' (Wyatt, R.J. (1991) 'Neuroleptics and the natural course of schizophrenia.' *Schizophrenia Bulletin 17*, 2).

(e) A study of 70 schizophrenia patients revealed that poorer outcome was associated with longer duration of untreated psychosis. Duration of psychotic symptoms was the only variable significantly associated with poorer outcome (Lieberman, J.A. *et al.* (1992) 'Prospective study of psychobiology in first-episode schizophrenia at Hillside Hospital.' *Schizophrenia Bulletin 18*, 3).

(f) Finally, Max Birchwood, clinical psychologist, and his colleagues claim that what is needed is a complementary approach, which focuses on the early phase of psychosis, with intervention strategies dedicated to 'what we have argued could be a critical period both biologically and psychosocially' (Birchwood, M., McGorry, P. and Jackson, H. (1997) 'Early intervention in schizophrenia.' *British Journal of Psychiatry 170*, 2–5).

(2) Acute problems: a survey of the quality of care in acute psychiatric wards

This survey was carried out by The Sainsbury Centre for Mental Health between September 1996 and April 1997. It involved 215 patients on nine acute psychiatric wards in different parts of the country. A free briefing paper, or the full report, at £9 plus 10 per cent p&p, can be obtained from The Sainsbury Centre for Mental Health, 134–138 Borough High Street, London SE1 1LB.

(3) Better Act Now!

A survey of the views of the NSF membership and staff on the quality of service provided by the system for those with a serious mental illness and their families, together with their recommendations for improvements. Approximately 2300 individuals participated in this. (Published by National Schizophrenia Fellowship (March 1999), *Better Act Now!* Campaign, Public Affairs, 30 Tabernacle Street, London EC2A 4DD.)

(4) An unannounced 'national visit' to acute psychiatric wards throughout England and Wales

A one-day survey of a stratified random sample which covered 47 per cent of the acute adult psychiatric inpatient units in England and Wales was carried out by officers of the Mental Health Act Commission in collaboration with the Sainsbury Mental Health Centre. This is reported in *British Medical Journal* (1998) *317*, 1279–1283 (Richard Ford, Graham Durcan, Lesley Warner, Pollyanna Hardy and Matt Muijen).

CHAPTER 2

Judgement rather than treatment and care?

As we noted in the first two books in this series, being admitted to hospital with a psychiatric problem does not necessarily mean that the underlying serious mental illness of the patient will be recognized and treated. Let us consider what happened to Julie.

CASE STUDY – PART 1[1]

Julie's 'A' level results were so good that she obtained a scholarship to help finance her studies at university and she went on to achieve a good honours degree. Contented and sociable, she was very much involved in college life and regularly wrote for the students' magazine. She had various other interests, including a love of music and playing several instruments. Her work came easily to her and when she later applied to do postgraduate study, one of her tutors enthusiastically supported this, summing Julie up as having a mature outlook and being courteous at all times.

During the summer after college finished, things started to go wrong. Julie later spoke of a sudden change, with everything feeling and looking different; it was as if something profound had happened to her – literally overnight – that she didn't understand. Later on, and very gradually, her parents and two sisters would also note changes in her. Almost imperceptibly she withdrew into herself, giving up her many interests and social activities one by one. She started going out for long walks on her own and slept very little. At one point, she complained to her elder sister that she had a voice in her head. Most

1   For Part 2 of this case study see Chapter 6.

untypically, Julie was also becoming destructive in the home, destroying valued possessions such as books and pictures.

As things deteriorated, it became clear that the young woman was depressed. When she started expressing suicidal ideas, her GP eventually arranged for her to be admitted to the psychiatric wing of a local hospital on a voluntary basis. Julie was put under constant observation and prescribed anti-depressants. Three weeks later, she was discharged from hospital. There was no improvement that her parents could see. They were by this time becoming very concerned and took their daughter to see a psychiatrist in a nearby city. Despite the fact that Julie seemed depressed and was hardly communicating at all with those around her, she talked to this doctor and complained about condemning voices in her head. This psychiatrist told the parents that he believed that their daughter was hallucinating and should be treated for a psychotic illness.

Shortly after this, Julie was back in hospital; this time the GP admitted her, again on a voluntary basis, because she was acting in a bizarre way in his surgery. She didn't like the ward and took to regularly walking several miles home. She was becoming increasingly destructive and the family started to hide away their books and pictures and other valued items. Most days, Julie spent much of her time at home in bed, sometimes laughing incongruously to herself. Meanwhile, her anti-depressants had been increased and weekly family meetings were held at the hospital. The now distraught parents expressed their anxieties and at two of these meetings they asked if their daughter could be psychotic. The psychiatrist and his team were adamant that this was not psychosis and that Julie's problem was behavioural and that she must learn to take responsibility for her destructive behaviour.

As things worsened – Julie had now been in hospital for two months, while continuing to spend much of her time at home – her parents asked several times for her to be detained under the Mental Health Act. They were told by hospital staff that she was not sectionable; even if she were to be sectioned she would appeal against it and a tribunal would take her off the section. Her GP even refused to consider seeking a mental health assessment when Julie was running around outside the house one evening with a large knife; once more the family were told that the young woman was not sectionable.

Around three months into this stay in hospital, and much to their relief, the family noted some improvement in Julie. She seemed to be calmer and making an effort to communicate with those around her. They realized what had happened very quickly when she complained that her legs were shaking and was given a 'side effect' drug for this; Julie had been put on anti-psychotic medication. However, the improvement was only very temporary because she suddenly refused to take the medication any longer. Once more, the young woman withdrew into herself, hardly communicating at all. At one point, however, she did complain to her family about her voices again and expressed suicidal ideas too.

Shortly, Julie's behaviour changed again and she became very disturbed and agitated, with a seeming need to talk incessantly. She started going out on long walks, taking nothing with her – no money or extra clothing – saying it helped with the voices. On one such occasion, the police found her walking on a motorway. They were sympathetic and understood why her parents wanted Julie to be kept in hospital under section. However, the hospital team continued to ignore their pleas.

The parents turned again to the psychiatrist from whom they had sought a second opinion and he immediately offered an NHS bed for Julie if a referral could be arranged. This was refused by Julie's psychiatrist. That same month, Julie tried to kill herself by overdosing. She spent a night in Casualty and was then sent back to hospital. A few days later, she damaged several cars outside the ward and by the time the police arrived she was mute. The police said she was too ill to be charged. Julie paid the hundreds of pounds needed to repair the damage. The hospital team continued to deny that there was anything seriously wrong with the young woman; they said that she knew what she was doing and was trying to 'get back' at her parents, but offered them no further explanation. Despite Julie's increasingly desperate behaviour and the fact that the psychiatrist who had offered her a bed had given his opinion that she had a serious mental illness, the consultant supervising her treatment maintained that his patient was making out that she was psychotic. Indeed, a nurse on the ward told Julie's mother that she did not have schizophrenia because she described voices inside her head rather than outside, so these weren't *real* hallucinations.

Six months after she was admitted to hospital, Julie was hardly eating or sleeping and taking long night walks on her own. She muttered to herself for hours on end but otherwise was mute. She looked haggard, with enormous staring, glazed eyes. She had lost interest in her appearance or hygiene. At this point, her mother happened to phone the ward and was told that her daughter was about to be discharged. This happened before any care plan was completed or a keyworker appointed. Julie was given an appointment to see the psychiatrist in six weeks time. Later when her mother protested that she was sure her daughter would be back, this time with the police, ward staff nodded in agreement. It seemed others were beginning to realize just how ill Julie might be after all.

Seven days later, Julie caused some damage in a neighbour's garden and returned to bed laughing to herself. Her mother asked the Social Services to arrange a mental health assessment. This was agreed and both the ASW and visiting psychiatrist felt the young woman was hallucinating but her GP again insisted she was not sectionable. In the following few days, Julie neither ate nor talked. She probably didn't sleep either, going out around dawn and returning later in the day. When at home she alternated between being destructive – destroying items around the house – or lying in bed staring into space for hours on end.

Twelve days after she was discharged from hospital, Julie threw bricks through several neighbours' windows and was arrested. The police were again sympathetic and seemed to be as astonished as her parents that she was not safely in hospital. This time, Julie was admitted to hospital under the Mental Health Act, by an ASW with the recommendations from a locum GP and a psychiatrist from the local hospital. Although Julie was meant to be under frequent and regular observation, a few days later her parents learned that their daughter had absconded. Before long she returned home and started smashing up the family furniture. Police took her back to hospital. This time she was put on a more secure ward and her 28-day Section 2 was converted to a 6-month Section 3. Just under one month later, she was put on the anti-psychotic drug which the psychiatrist who had seen her privately had recommended for her many months previously. A couple of months later, the psychiatrist who had constantly denied that his patient had a psychotic illness, now voiced an opinion that Julie might be suffering from schizophrenia. Nearly two years had passed since she had first started hallucinating and had struggled to cope with voices condemning her and urging her to kill herself. Meanwhile, she and her family had found themselves responsible for around two thousand pounds' worth of damage to property.

Julie was so disturbed by this time that it took another fifteen months in a specialist NHS resource, under the supervision of the psychiatrist who had previously offered her a bed, before she was stabilized on one of the 'new drugs'. Shortly after this, her mother was able to say delightedly that her daughter was becoming like her old self again – 'warm, spontaneous and rational'. She now hopes that the delays which took place before appropriate help was made available have not left Julie too vulnerable to further breakdown (1). Her mother also points out that during the time that she had no diagnosis, life was hell for Julie and the whole family. 'We were abused; tortured, really. But, why?', she asks.

COMMENT

This is one of those worrying cases where a sufferer has been under the supervision of mental health professionals for a considerable time without receiving a proper diagnosis or treatment. Julie's worsening condition was, it seems, put down to feigning a psychotic illness, reportedly motivated by a desire to 'get back at' a family to whom she nevertheless returned to at every opportunity. Why such an assessment should be reached and how this could be reconciled with the patient's 'pre-morbid' history remains a mystery.

Perhaps it would be helpful, before going on to read LEAP group's analysis and later discussion, to go back through this case study and make a note of anything that occurred which you believe could have persuaded the professionals that there may have been another explanation than the one they chose.

GROUP'S ANALYSIS OF THE CASE STUDY

It is not a surprise that the group was distressed by this young woman's experience and by the judgemental way in which she had been treated by both her GP and the hospital team. It seemed to members that there was no obvious reason why she should have been treated this way and they decided to explore this further.

A strange assessment

The LEAP group felt that most of what happened to Julie was inexcusable in the light of her recent past; she had been an active and productive student at university and had been very much involved in the life there. She was described as 'contented' and one of her tutors had proclaimed her to be mature in outlook as well as courteous at all times. As one carer pointed out, 'If anything, Julie seemed to be rather more adult than many young people of her age. Why was this ignored by the hospital team?'

Members felt there was no sense whatever in attempting to assess someone's mental health without taking into account their usual behaviour and lifestyle. One of them said 'It seems that they are content to look at the patient in a vacuum – how can anyone be assessed accurately on the basis of their behaviour at any one time without any backcloth to explain this?' 'Yes, as if the past doesn't count, which is nonsense!' another carer exclaimed.

'It's very unfair', a survivor agreed, 'If I'd been Julie, I'd have been mortified to have been treated this way – a really intelligent girl with a reputation for being courteous at all times. No wonder she slipped off home at every opportunity!'

First admission to hospital

The group could not understand what was meant to have been achieved during this first admission. As a carer pointed out, 'Seeing as there was no improvement in Julie's condition, why was she discharged after three weeks? It seems the parents were more worried about her at that point than before.'

Members felt this first admission would have been the right time to have hopefully come to grips with this illness. It was clear that Julie had been looking for help because she had 'opened up' and described her psychotic symptoms to the second psychiatrist. Had she also talked this way to anyone in the hospital, members wondered? 'Would they have understood what was happening if she had?' someone asked.

'This is so sad', a survivor observed, 'because Julie was telling how it really was for her; she was looking for and prepared to accept help at this stage, and that should have been a real bonus for the team working with her and not indicative of someone play-acting, or whatever!'

Second admission to hospital

By the time Julie went into hospital for a second time, she was exhibiting behavioural problems and becoming increasingly destructive. 'Why, then, was she still being treated only with anti-depressants?' wondered a carer, adding, 'I would have thought such behaviour would have had more to do with reacting to psychotic symptoms than with depression.' Yes, other members thought so too.

'Why did the hospital team decide her problem was 'behavioural' without first exploring the possibility that she might be psychotic?', a survivor, who is also a trained mental health professional, wanted to know, adding, 'Why look for deviance rather than illness? They knew she was depressed. And why were they actually increasing her anti-depressants while denying she was ill?'

'And why didn't they listen to these parents at all?' asked a carer, 'not only did they refuse to consider a psychotic illness being the problem, but they also refused their requests to consider sectioning their daughter as well.' 'Yes', agreed another, 'and I don't see how they could do this in the circumstances; they could hardly claim Julie wasn't ill when they'd already kept her in hospital two months, could they? She should have been sectioned "in the interests of her health" at this stage if only to provide a proper chance to observe her instead of her going off home all the time.' This, of course, is a reference to the fact that the Mental Health Act 1983 allows for sectioning someone to protect their health from further deterioration. 'That's right,' agreed a survivor, 'if she needed to be in hospital, she needed to be there and not running home every day.'

At this point, a carer who has taken a real interest in the workings of the law asked, 'and, what is this nonsense about Julie not being sectionable because she would appeal against it and a tribunal would take her off the section? The team had no right to use this as an excuse for not attempting to arrange a section for a patient; it's not their job to forecast what a tribunal might or might not do.'

The GP's interpretation of the mental health law

The group noted that Julie's GP seemed to be more in accord with the hospital team than with his patient and that he actually refused the parents' request for her to have a mental health assessment when, still a hospital patient, she was running around outside her home with a large knife. No-one had any doubts at all that this was an insupportable decision; the young woman was clearly very disturbed at this point and could well have been a danger to herself or others. As members pointed out, one of the grounds for sectioning under the Mental Health Act 1983 is concerned with the safety of the patient and other people. 'Anyway, both the GP and the hospital team seem to have missed the point, don't they?' a survivor pointed out, 'The point of a mental health assessment is to determine whether or not someone is sectionable. It is not the GP's place – nor a ward team's for that matter – to make such a decision without the use of this tool.'

A brief respite

The group noted that at this point – just as things had been getting out of hand – Julie started to calm down and to communicate with those around her. It seems that she was being prescribed anti-psychotic medication at this stage, although the parents were left to work this out for themselves. How could the hospital team have missed the significant change in her at this point? Members asked what was the point of putting her on different medication if they didn't then properly observe the results of this? 'Well, even if they did, they couldn't do anything about it when she refused to take the medication any longer without applying for her to be sectioned,' a carer pointed out, 'and they'd made it very clear they were determined not to do that, hadn't they?'

Members felt that things could only get worse at this point and they did. It seemed to them quite incredible that no attempt was made to section the young woman when she started going on long, lonely walks and when she was found by the police on a motorway.

A second opinion

The group found it quite unacceptable that Julie's psychiatrist refused to refer her on to the second psychiatrist. His patient's condition was worsening all the time. Meanwhile, he was claiming that she was feigning illness and was trying to 'get back' at her parents, while offering no explanation for this opinion. A survivor asked 'What vested interest did this psychiatrist have in refusing this referral? He must have been very confident in his own judgment to ignore the opinions of another psychiatrist, the family and the police and also the fact that his patient was now deteriorating fast, so what did he have to lose?' 'Yes,' agreed a carer, 'the police are used to dealing with bad behaviour and it seems they made it clear throughout this case that they shared the parents' concern about Julie, even declaring her too ill to be charged at one point.'

A second carer was genuinely perplexed; she wanted to know why anyone would pretend to be psychotic? 'Can anyone think of one benefit to be had by doing this?' she asked. 'No', laughed a survivor, 'it beggars belief, doesn't it?' The group were so concerned about this aspect of the case that they decided to take a further look at this phenomenon later.

Discharge

Members found it very difficult to take in that this psychiatrist could now discharge his patient – when she was so clearly more ill than ever – after refusing to refer her to a psychiatrist who was offering her a bed. 'We used to call this a "dog in the manger" attitude when I was a child, but his actions are rather more serious than this, aren't they?' mused a carer. 'They certainly are; they're quite chilling, in fact', agreed a survivor. 'And while we're on the subject, why isn't every patient entitled to a second opinion, as of right?' Members weren't sure but one or two suspected that this could be arranged if their GP agrees to it. 'If that's the case, Julie didn't stand a chance', a mother grunted in disgust. The view of the LEAP group was that a second opinion should be a legal right for every patient.

'Meanwhile,' a survivor pointed out, 'she's then discharged without a care plan or keyworker.' 'Yes, and it would be stretching the imagination after what we've heard in this case to believe this was due to a sudden shortage of beds, wouldn't it?' a carer suggested, adding, 'I mean, when they can keep someone in hospital for so long and let her go home every day!' 'But', exclaimed a second survivor, 'how – after being so long in hospital – can a patient who is mute, not eating or sleeping and being violent towards other people's property be discharged and sent home without any support?' This just about summed up the LEAP group's view of the situation.

The GP's interpretation of the law revisited

Members noted that once again Julie's GP refused to accept she might be sectionable even when an ASW and a psychiatrist felt she was hallucinating after causing damage in a neighbour's garden. 'And she was so ill following this – if I'd been Julie's parent, I'd have been tempted to call him out during the night a few times. I don't think he should have been allowed to turn his back on this family at a time like this!' exclaimed a mother who could well identify with the dilemma Julie's parents found themselves in. Another carer voiced his thoughts more plainly, 'Is this GP nuts or something?' adding, 'couldn't the ASW have done something about his attitude?'

Members weren't sure but it seemed to them that there wasn't really anything the ASW could have done about this because two medical recommendations were required for the section to take place and the second doctor might well have accepted the GP's opinion as Julie was his patient. 'Yes,' someone commented, 'We shouldn't be surprised that Julie was finally sectioned when neither her psychiatrist nor her GP were available, should we? It was going to take an assessment by professionals without any preconceived notions about this poor girl for anything to be achieved!'

A third admission to hospital

Members were relieved that once Julie had been brought back to the hospital after absconding, she was now protected from herself and her illness by being put on a secure ward and given time, with a six months section, to start to get better. They found it laughable that her psychiatrist was prepared to entertain the idea that she might have schizophrenia two months after she was put on an anti-psychotic drug and nearly two years after she had first started hallucinating. 'I can't see his opinion was worth anything at all by this time, can you?' a survivor asked, 'Unless, of course, this would mean the family would get their money back for the damage his patient had caused under his care?' she added grimly. 'Oh, I wish!' exclaimed another survivor. Unfortunately, this didn't seem remotely likely.

Members of the LEAP group decided there was nothing to be gained by pursuing this analysis any further; they couldn't find anything positive in this case study to comment on apart from the moral support the family had received from the police throughout their ordeal (2).

The LEAP group was amazed at the emphasis put on the behavioural content of Julie's illness and the fact that this could be interpreted as pretending to be psychotic.

Feigning illness

Members could not remember coming across a case where this has cropped up before. One survivor could not get over Julie being labelled in this way. 'I thought everyone understood that the aggression we show when we're psychotic is all about frustration!' she exclaimed. 'A sign of not being able to cope with all that is going on in your head. Can you imagine what it does to anyone who is being condemned by voices in their head to be told they must learn to take responsibility for their bad behaviour?' 'Yes, it's like being punished by yourself and then punished again by the people who should be helping you!' agreed another survivor. A third member joined in with 'Once when I was told I was being "attention-seeking" and I had all this blame and guilt going around in my head, I just became more angry and destructive towards myself. I could weep for Julie – she kept trying to tell them what it was like for her, didn't she, but apparently her's weren't the right kind of voices for that team!'

Another concern for members was that this seemed to be a 'Catch 22' situation. It seemed that any evidence of psychotic symptoms, including whatever the sufferer might offer in moments of insight, could be dismissed as increasingly perfect feigning of such an illness! Someone summed this up with, 'Yes, the quandary for unsuspecting and deserving new sufferers is quite awesome! And crazier than any psychosis!'

On a lighter note, members agreed that it would seem very reasonable to suppose that anyone who believed that there was anything to gain by pretending to be psychotic would have to be at least a little mad – at least two survivors felt this to be something of an understatement. Any attempt to make it a behavioural quirk rather than illness was therefore null and void!

So why focus on behaviour rather than illness?

While working on this series, members of the LEAP group have had reason to ask this question several times. It sometimes seems that a lot of professional time and energy is spent on avoiding a diagnosis of serious mental illness until this eventually becomes inevitable. As a carer pointed out, 'We hear so much about the scarcity of resources – and goodness knows we could do with some more out in the community to help keep people well – but how come management don't seem to be too concerned about all the wastage of resources which takes place when sufferers are in hospital? Can you begin to imagine how much must have been spent on Julie by now because she was allowed to become so very ill instead of having appropriate treatment?' 'Quite,' a survivor agreed, 'and I don't believe we'll see much change until those who pay for the services start to look at this side of the equation. Then, perhaps, good practice will be recognized.'

It is perhaps not surprising that research over the past two decades is now confirming the logical view that conditions such as schizophrenia are no different to other illness; early intervention is paramount when it comes to prognosis (1). So, how is it that individuals like Julie can be under the supervision of mental health professionals for so long without receiving a proper diagnosis and appropriate treatment? Why, as a survivor in the group asked earlier, 'look for deviance rather than illness?'

A legacy from the 1960s

At this point a carer observed, with a sigh, 'It seems to me that a lot of those working with the mentally ill have never moved on from the 1960s when the anti-psychiatry movement became fashionable. You know, there's no such thing as mental illness.' 'That's right,' another agreed, 'and the logical progression from that was that if someone was diagnosed as having schizophrenia they were being scapegoated – usually because they were making a nuisance of themselves to society or, more likely, their families!' 'Yes, and then everyone with nothing better to do produced theories to fit these ideas, didn't they?' someone else joined in. 'What with labelling theories (3) and family theories (4), who needed medicine?'

'Perhaps the most important point in all of this', a survivor responded quietly, 'was that other professionals had the chance to distance themselves from medicine and the medical hierarchy, didn't they?'

An abundance of theories and approaches

Yes, the group thought she was probably right about this professional distancing being the most important outcome of what happened to psychiatry in the 1960s; as a direct result of this, there was a determined drive by the social work and nursing professionals to separate themselves from the 'medical model'.

The late R.D. Laing – a psychiatrist who blamed society, and families in particular, for something psychiatry called 'schizophrenia' – became the guru of social work training courses. Meanwhile, student nurses were encouraged to look at the whole individual – and in particular their presenting behaviour – rather than focus on a diagnosis. The word 'schizophrenia' started disappearing from their examination papers at a time when more hospital beds were still used by patients with this illness than any other.

'Yes, and perhaps even more important, lots of psychiatrists were left feeling quite ambivalent about their "medical model" of serious mental illness and even some of those who knew their approach was still very valid were nevertheless apologetic about this!' a carer joined in. 'And add to all this the fact that many of those now at the top of their various professions trained in the 1960s and 1970s. It's not difficult to see why the jury is still out on serious mental illness, is it?' was the wry comment of another carer.

It is arguable that this sort of rivalry among professions and the legacy of many of today's senior professionals having trained during the years when psychiatry was rubbished, has led to an extraordinary situation where any one sufferer's illness may be treated in a variety of ways on a continuum running from 'disturbed behaviour' through to 'psychosis'. The LEAP group feels that Julie's experience demonstrates this quite clearly. They also believe that it clarifies the need for an independent second opinion to be available as a right for all patients.

A second opinion revisited

As one member put it, 'there is something very wrong when the opinion of another doctor can be ignored, and later his offer of a specialist NHS bed refused, just prior to the patient being discharged from hospital when she is critically ill.' 'Well, yes, a situation such as this suggests that we have a system which is more concerned with protecting the right of a – hopefully – minority of ineffective doctors to "play God" than with protecting the interests of seriously ill patients!' was another member's opinion. 'And it's not as if there is just one approach to the treating of this type of illness, is it?' a survivor exclaimed, 'So, we're all stepping around on the edge of a minefield each time we get ill. Surely we should at least have the right to say "I want a psychiatrist who believes in treating psychosis as an illness". Isn't that right?'

The LEAP group had no doubts that this is how it should be but, as someone pointed out, 'as most NHS psychiatrists work in catchment areas, there's no way this could be made to work. But, then, that just makes it more imperative that every patient should have the right to an independent second opinion, doesn't it?'

SUMMING UP

The group felt that a number of issues had been raised in this case study. These included a now familiar ignorance about the law and its purpose (see the second book in this series, *Mental Health Assessments*); the need for a proper assessment to take account of the sufferer's 'pre-morbid' personality and the family's experience of her; and the need for an automatic right to a second opinion, particularly in view of the existing variations in approach to serious mental illness.

Finally, members searched for any signs of compassion and respect for the patient either in the GP or in this hospital team and found none.

INFORMATION

The following pieces of information are relevant to points brought up during the group's analysis and discussion which have been highlighted in the text:

(1) The importance of early intervention in a schizophrenic illness

(a) A large extended study of first episodes of schizophrenia revealed that the most important determinant of future relapses was the duration of illness prior to starting neuroleptic medication (Crow, T.J. *et al.* (1986) 'The Northwick Park study of first episodes of schizophrenia, part II: A randomized controlled trial of prophylactic neuroleptic treatment.' *British Journal of Psychiatry 148*, 120–127).

(b) Not long after the above survey was published, workers conducting a follow-up study of schizophrenia across North America, claimed that it may take only one year of active illness for deterioration or a 'threshold of chronicity' to be reached (McGlashan, T.H. (1988) 'A selective review of recent North American long-term follow-up studies of schizophrenia.' *Schizophrenia Bulletin 14*, 4, 515–542).

(c) A Tokyo University study showed that patients who had had symptoms longer than 1 year before entering treatment were more likely to relapse than patients who were treated within the year (Anzai, N. *et al.* (1988) 'Early neuroleptic medication within one year after onset can reduce risk of later relapses in schizophrenic patients.' *Annual Report Pharmacopsychiatric Research Foundation 19*, 258–265).

(d) Richard Jed Wyatt has concluded, in his comprehensive overview of the use of neuroleptic medication and the natural course of schizophrenia, that 'some patients are left with a damaging residual if a psychosis is allowed to proceed unmitigated. While psychosis is undoubtedly demoralising and stigmatising, it may also be biologically toxic' (Wyatt, R.J. (1991) 'Neuroleptics and the natural course of schizophrenia.' *Schizophrenia Bulletin 17*, 2).

(e) A study of 70 schizophrenia patients revealed that poorer outcome was associated with longer duration of untreated psychosis. Duration of psychotic symptoms was the only variable significantly associated with poorer outcome (Lieberman, J.A. *et al.* (1992) 'Prospective study of psychobiology in first-episode schizophrenia at Hillside Hospital.' *Schizophrenia Bulletin 18*, 3).

(f)   Finally, Max Birchwood, clinical psychologist, and colleagues claim
      that what is needed is a complementary approach, which focuses on
      the early phase of psychosis, with intervention strategies dedicated to
      'what we have argued could be a critical period both biologically
      and psychosocially' (Birchwood, M., McGorry, P. and Jackson, H.
      (1997) 'Early intervention in schizophrenia.' *British Journal of
      Psychiatry 170*, 2–5).

(2) The role of the police

It is common for families seeking help for a mentally ill relative to
praise the work of the police. A National Schizophrenia Fellowship
survey carried out on behalf of the Department of Health revealed
that among the 563 carers who took part, the police were the most
highly rated service when it came to caring for the mentally ill.
Provision of Community Services for Mentally Ill People and their Carers
(1990), NSF.

An earlier unpublished survey of 889 National Schizophrenia
Fellowship members gives perhaps some indication as to why
carers might feel this way. One of the findings revealed that 161
sufferers obtained no help for their first episode of a serious
mental illness until the police intervened (Mary Tyler 1986).

(3) Labelling theories

During the 1960s, the heyday of the anti-psychiatry movement,
labelling theories became immensely popular with academics and
health professionals. In simple terms, the theory is that (a) when it
suits a society to do so, it scapegoats those who make a nuisance of
themselves and give them a label and (b) this label then becomes a
self-fulfilling prophecy.

The way this is meant to work in practice is that a diagnosis of a
serious mental illness is nothing more than a label, with
psychiatrists using labelling for their own ends (which were never
quite clear). The patients they dealt with were the 'presenting
patients', ie, the individuals scapegoated by 'sick' families for all
their supposed problems. It is perhaps not at all surprising that
these extreme ideas were eventually discarded and discredited
during the 1970s, they did however leave a legacy of a pro-
nounced reluctance to diagnose a serious mental illness, ie 'we
must not label people with something as serious as this'. By
implication, of course, this can mean no diagnosis and, worse,

no explanations about how to deal with it. This is the main reason for so many patients and their families having to try to cope with what has happened to them without any of the information that they need if they are to do this successfully.

It is interesting that in *Getting into the System* (pp.21 and 22) members of the LEAP group with personal experience of a serious mental illness pointed out that the problem is not about getting a label; it's about *not knowing your label* although it's on the medical file and can be passed to various authorities while patient and family are still unaware of what the diagnosis is!

(4) Family theories

During the 1960s and 1970s there was an abundance of theories of a similar kind which blamed the families of schizophrenia sufferers for their relative's illness. These popular ideas dominated much of the literature and received wisdom of the time and added significantly to the misery of families trying to cope with living with a serious mental illness.

Long since discredited and abandoned, because, among other things, researchers were discovering for the first time the idiosyncrasies of normal family life rather than anything unusual about families coping with schizophrenia, they have nevertheless influenced for many years the attitudes of some of those who in turn have influence over the training and supervision of recruits to the caring professions; readers interested in this phenomenon may like to read Christine Heron's chapter on mental health carers in *Working with Carers*, 1998. London: Jessica Kingsley Publishers.

For a full discussion and useful references on the family theories, see Gwen Howe (1991) *The Reality of Schizophrenia*. London: Faber & Faber, pp.79–81.

EXERCISE

You are a student who has been encouraged to write a thesis on various approaches to the diagnosis and treatment of psychosis. On one ward, you are introduced to Julie and told she has been there for six months and is suspected of feigning a psychotic illness. What sort of questions do you think you might like to ask (a) the ward team and (b) the patient?

CHAPTER 3

An introduction to serious mental illness

It appears that some hospital teams see no reason to communicate with their patients, or those closest to them, even during a first episode of a serious mental illness. Naomi and her husband describe what happened to them in their own words.

CASE STUDY – PART 1[1]

My experience of getting information about my wife's illness
'Naomi was first admitted to a psychiatric hospital following a period of very odd behaviour for her. After years of a close and happy relationship she suddenly turned against me. She had suffered with bouts of lows and highs for several months and our GP eventually referred her to a psychiatrist. We were given no explanations and things suddenly got worse with Naomi becoming very excited and expressing bizarre religious ideas. By chance, after having no sleep for three days and nights, Naomi was due to see the psychiatrist again. When I realized this I was very relieved but couldn't see how I could persuade my wife to keep this appointment.

'I needed somebody's help as I had just returned from the Accident and Emergency department of the local hospital with a dislocated shoulder, my arm in a sling and suffering from mild concussion. I had collapsed down the stairs head first after having tried to stay awake for the past three days and nights, chasing around after Naomi, trying to prevent her from coming to harm. She seemed to be unaware of everyday dangers such as traffic on the roads and was frantically on the go every moment of the day and night. When I first

1   For Part 3 of this case study see Chapter 6

regained consciousness upside down on the stairs with blood running from my head, my first thought was to get help for my wife. My second thought was one of enormous relief that just for a short time I need not look after her twenty-four hours a day; somebody else would have to do it! My third thought was a feeling of guilt for thinking this way. But I did so need a rest! First, though, I needed to get to hospital; I couldn't lie here indefinitely.

'Somehow, between us, we managed to get an ambulance and once I was sorted out and back home, a phone call brought my brother, Steve, round to our home to see what he could do to help. As he gradually begun to understand that something was very wrong, he took over and somehow persuaded Naomi to come to the hospital with us that morning. When the psychiatrist saw the state she was in, she asked Naomi to come back and see her in the afternoon – presumably for a mental health assessment, but we were never told.

'No-one made any attempt to help my brother and I cope with my wife's increasingly excited and bizarre behaviour while we waited for this second interview with the doctor. Somehow, Steve managed to keep Naomi in the hospital and to help both of us get to this appointment. When we entered the room, there were several people sitting there, although we were not introduced to them, and they quickly made it clear to her that they wanted Naomi to remain in the hospital. She did not want to stay and tried to run. Nobody attempted to stop her. Steve, who was waiting for us outside the door, eventually persuaded my wife to stay. This included physically restraining her at one point. This must have been very difficult for both of them at the time and subsequently.

'I assume that Naomi must have been placed under the necessary detention order around now (we were told nothing about this nor about our rights under the Mental Health Act) as she was pinned down by nursing staff who gave her an injection without explaining to her what was going on. I know Naomi found this the most frightening and humiliating experience of her life. How could she be expected to trust and respect the nurses and doctors after that?

'My wife was admitted to a hospital ward where my grandmother had died not long ago after several years of being treated for some kind of dementia. This was my only previous experience of mental illness. I had no reason at that stage, or for nearly another week, to assume that Naomi would ever come out of hospital either.

'I found it very confusing working out who were patients and who were nurses on the ward as the latter did not wear uniform – just very casual clothes – and did not approach visitors when they entered the ward. Obviously, with each change of shift, there was a change of staff and I had great difficulty sorting out who was who. When I did, I wasn't able to find out from any of the staff team what Naomi's diagnosis or prognosis was, despite my visiting every day and asking them what was wrong with her and what they were doing for her and also telephoning and asking them the same questions in between visits. They would just say that she needed to be in hospital; it was the best place for her. However, this did not appear to be carried out in practice as she went out shopping unsupervised and went to the pub in the evening with fellow patients, also unsupervised, and with no guidance as to whether she should drink alcohol despite her hospital administered medication (1). She continued to be oblivious to the dangers of passing traffic when crossing the busy local roads. In short, she was not capable at that point of looking after herself.

'Several days passed and I was working out the practical implications of Naomi being permanently in hospital. When was it best to visit if this was now to be a routine part of my life? How would I tell our friends and family? How would I ensure she had clean clothes every day? Would she be better somewhere else? I now know that at this stage one of my aunts told my mother that they could both sell their houses and buy a big house in the country where we could keep Naomi as best as we could. A bit reminiscent of Jane Eyre perhaps, but with the kindest of intentions! It was not only me who was in the dark about what to do.

'My brother was a great help during this period, ensuring that I ate and taking me to the hospital as my shoulder prevented me from driving. Partly because of my physical and mental exhaustion, I was more resigned to the situation than he was. Steve pointed out that as nothing seemed to be being done at the hospital and nobody we spoke to there seemed to know anything, he suggested getting a second opinion. For example, could they operate on her brain if it was a tumour which was affecting Naomi's behaviour? I agreed it might be a good idea to get a second opinion and we arranged for a private consultant to come to the hospital. He sat down and talked with Naomi and myself, separately, and at length. After this, he told me, 'I agree with the diagnosis.' 'What diagnosis?' I exclaimed. He told me that my wife had been diagnosed as having MD, ie manic depression or, if I found it easier, a bi-polar affective disorder. He explained about the illness and told me that the prognosis for many was good. He was like a quiet breath of fresh air and sunshine in my haze of uncertainty and ignorance. I found out later that Naomi was more informed than me by this stage; she had compared her symptoms with somebody else in the ward who had MD!

'I was very surprised to immediately feel nothing but enormous relief at having a diagnosis, however serious; having an explanation for Naomi's strange behaviour. It wasn't that she had just decided to change, to have strange thoughts and to hate me. I was not to blame for the lack of understanding that had now come between us, destroying so much of the fun and friendship that we had previously shared. There was a reason for all this. The reason was MD. I could now find out about this illness. I could read about it, about what helped and what didn't help. Should we avoid certain things? Who had the necessary expertise to guide us?

'*I started to hope.* Might it be possible that some of Naomi's love, understanding, patience and wisdom – the wife I knew and loved – would return? Might we one day be able to sit quietly in our garden together as we used to on warm summer evenings? Might we go out for a meal together again? Might we even be able to consider a holiday of some sort, perhaps stay in the Lake District as we used to? Yes, now there was hope. Despite having supportive and caring family and friends, I had felt so helpless and isolated up until then. But now there was hope again because of a diagnosis and somebody telling us what that diagnosis was!'

PART 2

My immediate experience of life after diagnosis – Naomi takes up the story.

'Looking back, I realize that both Ron and I were at an enormous disadvantage whilst, for whatever reason, my diagnosis was being withheld from us. Not being told my diagnosis meant that neither of us were able to find out what was happening to me. We didn't know I had MD and therefore we were not able to try to understand it and cope with it. Moreover, this also meant that we were denied the knowledge that I might recover from my illness. Ron's notes sum up very well the unnecessary distress caused by me not being told about my diagnosis. Even when I was told as a result of calling in an outside consultant, the staff in the hospital to which I had been admitted did not offer any information about the illness. But, then, neither was their any sort of welcome when I arrived nor an explanation of procedure on the ward.

'I was in a place where it seemed to me there was no optimism that people were expected to recover. The staff always seemed to be busy elsewhere; they avoided our questions and many of them appeared to be disinterested. We got the impression that staff never passed messages and never spoke to each other about their patients or their illnesses. In fact, if degrees were awarded for evading questions and ignoring patients there would have been several staff on this ward who were candidates deserving first class honours!

'There was little therapy apart from the drug treatment. The only occupational therapy that I observed during my week on this ward was being allowed to wander, unsupervised into town. I went to the shops and to the local pub with the full knowledge of the staff, but was given no advice about my medication and how drinking alcohol might affect me. All this was at a time when I was seriously deluded and I still thought I was Jesus.

'Often I felt threatened by other people in the ward. I was actually threatened by one 'tough' girl whose pen I had used without permission. Although I was high at the time, this didn't stop me being frightened by her but it did lead to inappropriate responses and I nearly got romantically involved with a male patient and gave him some presents. However, there seemed to be no attempt to protect me from myself and my illness (2). It was as if first-time patients could get on and learn from experience despite their very real vulnerability.

'The decoration and furnishings in the wards were poorly maintained and therefore had become tatty and dirty. Somebody urinated on the floor of the ward and this was not cleared up until many hours later. Another lady had been given a bed in the corner of the dining room where we used to sit with our visitors and a part of her illness meant that she often took off her nightdress during visiting times. There were lots of hard surfaces and faded gloss paint and most areas had peculiar, unpleasant smells. For me and my visitors, it was not a place in which one felt one could easily get better from a serious mental illness! I now know that Ron was very unhappy that I was in such a dismal pace, without any tangible benefits for me that he could see. It seemed I had been put there while my illness was making me a nuisance. A sort of detention without therapy!'

COMMENT

Perhaps it is not surprising that following this, their first experience of the system, Naomi and Ron now devote much of their spare time trying to make it easier for others who follow in their wake.

It might be worthwhile before proceeding to the group's analysis to pause for a moment to consider at what stages during the development and flare up of Naomi's illness you believe you would have welcomed explanations, advice or support if you had been her husband.

GROUP'S ANALYSIS OF THE CASE STUDY

Members of the group were sad to read about this couple's introduction to the mental health services. They decided to follow their example by dividing this analysis into two parts, first dealing with the carer's and then the sufferer's experience.

A developing illness

It appeared to the group that Ron really learned nothing about what was happening to his wife during the months leading up to her crisis. Several members brought up this matter as they felt it was quite unnecessary to leave him and his wife in complete ignorance as to what might be happening to her. One commented, 'It was remiss of the psychiatrist not to give them both some sort of explanation about what might be happening. If they had, then Ron and his family would not have been left later fretting about conditions like dementia and brain tumours.'

Everyone agreed that some sort of explanation was needed from the time of Naomi's first appointment with the psychiatrist, although this was obviously too soon for a precise diagnosis. As it was, Ron had no understanding about the dramatic changes taking place in his wife or how he should deal with them. This put the couple at a profound disadvantage right from the start.

A chapter of accidents

There were rueful grins as members discussed Ron's own catastrophe in falling down the stairs one night during Naomi's crisis and injuring himself quite badly. As one carer put it, 'If you get tired enough and desperate enough you just don't know what you're doing any more. I've been there, but not in quite such a devastating way as this!'

Members could also identify with Ron's racing thoughts as he lay on the stairs partly concussed; first, what could he do about his wife, second, thank goodness someone else would have to sort that out now, and third, guilt at feeling relieved at the thought! They also wondered what would have happened if Steve hadn't been available to help the couple? 'Just how would Ron have got Naomi to the hospital, and stopped her leaving before and during the second interview if he had had to cope on his own?' demanded a carer.

Some of the carers in the group often muse about the lack of urgency demonstrated by everyone except themselves when their relative is in crisis. The psychiatrist's actions once Naomi arrived for her morning appointment against all the odds struck them as being a very good example of this complacency in the face of potential disaster for someone else. 'In fact, it's a case of hooray for Steve!' a survivor observed, adding, 'I suspect Ron's neighbours or anyone passing by in the street would have taken more interest in his predicament than the staff seemed to at this hospital!' Yes, the group was more than a little surprised that no-one seemed to comment on Ron's state when he turned up at the hospital clearly wounded as well as stunned, either then, or later, during his visits to see her on the ward. 'It almost seems that he didn't exist for any of the professionals concerned, doesn't it?' suggested another survivor. The group was used to commenting on the way sufferer's families are too often ignored but this particular instance seemed to them to be quite bizarre as well as uncaring.

A denial of rights?

One aspect of this case study had everyone confused. It did seem that the psychiatrist arranged the second interview in order to have Naomi assessed for admission under the Mental Health Act and that the couple have always assumed this was the case, particularly as she was forcibly given an injection shortly after the interview ended. However, there is no other evidence to this effect and neither sufferer nor carer were informed of their rights under the legislation. Someone in the group wondered why the couple had never sought clarification on this from the hospital? Another member proposed that perhaps so much time had passed before they learned about such matters that this particular aspect of Naomi's admission had little importance for them? Either way, although it did seem that here was cause for complaint, members were really more disturbed about Naomi's first experience of the nursing staff causing her so much distress.

A survivor wondered 'If Naomi was so disturbed at the time, did the staff feel she wouldn't understand an explanation?' adding after a pause, 'but, if so, they should still have attempted one or at least told her what they were about to do, shouldn't they?' 'That's right,' agreed a second survivor, 'and they should then have returned to the subject as soon as she was ready for this. Any such attempt at communication would have registered later, if not at the time. Instead, Naomi looks back on this as an assault and it's not really surprising, is it?'

'It makes you wonder whether professionals understand how much awareness one can have while suffering a high, doesn't it?' mused another survivor. 'Perhaps they don't realize we can remember a lot of the detail of a manic episode? Nothing else would seem to explain the lack of follow-up and explanations after this "assault" so far as I can see!' The group felt this was an important point, worthy of note for those working with MD.

Confusion on the wards

Members were interested in Ron's comments about his confusion at finding that the staff were not easily identifiable on the ward. It seemed to them that this subject comes up repeatedly.

'We could be forgiven for believing that it's only the nurses who are happy with this situation, couldn't we?' muttered a carer, at which point a mother burst out laughing and told us 'When I walked into the ward after my son was admitted the second time, I was met by a man at the door who asked me who I wanted to see and who then took me to my son in the men's dormitory. I was later told that the man was a patient and that I was not meant to be in the dormitory.' When she added that no-one saw them go up there, someone else pointed out, 'It makes you realize how slack security must be when no-one really knows who anyone else is, doesn't it?' 'Well, that's right,' laughed a survivor, 'otherwise, how could a visitor be taken up to the dormitory by a business-like stranger who turns out to be a patient while other visitors wander about the ward aimlessly trying to track down members of staff or the patient they've come to see?'

Burden of worry

Members agreed that Ron's description of what happened during Naomi's first week in hospital made it quite clear that he was left to become increasingly agitated about what had happened. Despite his persistent demands for some sort of explanation, he was left to believe he might have lost the wife he knew for ever. Nevertheless, members did agree with a carer who pointed out that it might take the psychiatrist more than a few days to reach a diagnosis of MD because of the need to first eliminate other possible explanations. Furthermore, another member pointed out that it is frequently the case that ward staff are told by the supervising doctor not to discuss such matters with the patient or family. Either way, she pointed out, this could have meant that ward staff could not give Ron any answers. While other members could see that was certainly quite possible, the general feeling was that it wasn't so much a definite diagnosis that was needed during those first few days as Ron being given the chance to ask questions, to express his fears and to receive some reassurance on these.

As one survivor exclaimed, 'I can't believe that someone so caring and obviously worried to distraction could not have been sat down and given some sort of explanation!' and this summed up the general feeling of the group. She went on to claim 'As it is, there should be some kind of mediator to help carers in a situation like this.' This suggestion met with the immediate approval of other members who realized just how helpful this could have been for a man besotted with worry and still dazed from the after-effects of a nasty accident. They decided to return to this topic in their later discussion.

A duty to care and protect

It seemed singularly unfortunate to members that the only sort of explanation given to Ron was that his wife needed to be in hospital. They had no doubt that was an accurate assessment, 'but the poor man knew his wife was going out and about in the town blithely unaware of the dangers of traffic and – if she had been so inclined – to drink as much alcohol as she pleased in the local pub!' someone pointed out. There seemed to be no doubt that members felt that this sort of freedom, even encouragement – as other patients seemed to go out to the pub too – for Naomi to take such risks was inexcusable. As one mother put it, 'There should be supervision for patients while they are very vulnerable. It was the same with my son. You think that at last they are safely in hospital. Wrong! It's not necessarily so!'

A diagnosis

No-one was at all surprised to learn how Ron felt when he was told his wife's diagnosis, together with a careful, positive, explanation. The LEAP group's experience has constantly been that sufferers and carers usually say they started to cope at the time when they learned the diagnosis, and thus the means to find out all about it and the chance to meet with others who 'have been there'.

Members felt that Ron described very well the transition from grief and a real sense of bereavement to feelings of relief and the right to hope again once the doctor told him what was the matter with his wife. They felt this description could be very useful for training purposes; that it might help service providers to better understand the needs of those who love someone with a serious mental illness.

As the group moved on to the sufferer's point of view about all this, they noted that Naomi also put a lot of emphasis on the need to know the diagnosis and, indeed, to know that she might recover from her illness. A survivor pointed out that even at the point that she did learn she had MD, nobody in the hospital offered Naomi any information about this, adding 'I think this is very sad and it does rather suggest that no-one was interested in helping a first-time sufferer, period!'

Staff involvement with patients

Members did not seem too surprised at Naomi's comments about staff evading questions and ignoring patients, and – so far as she could gather – failing to monitor them effectively too. One carer said grimly, 'At the hospital my son goes into, you often find most of the staff in the office or sitting with the same few patients when you visit. I know I am not the only one to feel this because when friends visit him on the ward they come back saying the same thing and are quite amazed at the lack of interaction between the ward staff and most of the patients.'

There was general agreement from members that this is the case more often than not. Someone said, 'Yes, staff can be found lounging around reading a newspaper or sitting laughing and joking in the office while patients sit staring into space', and a survivor nodded in agreement. Although there may be justified reasons, at times, for a lack of staff involvement with patients, it is interesting to note that a survey has revealed that when Mental Health Act Commissioners made an unannounced visit to acute psychiatric wards in England and Wales one November morning in 1996 they found no nurses interacting with patients on 26 per cent of these wards (3).

This all seemed rather depressing and at this point someone suggested that the group should bear in mind that most of its members have had experience of individual nurses whose dedication is inspiring. Yes, others agreed this was certainly so and particularly the case, it seemed, out in the community. What they found worrying, however, was that on some wards it did seem as though staff teams had somehow 'lost the plot'. One survivor said wearily, 'Naomi's point about not even being given a welcome when she arrived nor any explanation about the procedure of the ward really sums it all up, doesn't it?' 'Yes,' another agreed, 'it seems that the nurses don't seem to have a specific role or proper framework to function in. Lots of them seem to be bored beyond words and I can quite understand why. There can't be much job satisfaction under these circumstances, can there?'

A lack of stimulation

Group members felt that the lack of any occupational therapy reported by Naomi might explain – but not justify – patients being allowed to wander round the town or go to the pub. As one carer said, 'We seem to have lost much of the knowledge that even the Victorians had about mental illness; they did at least realize that having something to do does help someone with a tormented mind.' Yes, a well educated survivor who has continued to study much of her adult life agreed with this. She told us that when there was an occupational therapy department in her local hospital, she used to appreciate the enthusiastic encouragement given her by occupational therapists to try out new skills, adding 'I used to feel very pleased with myself when I mastered something new and had something to show for my stay in hospital. It's a shame this doesn't seem to happen any more.'

No-one had any doubts she was right. Members find that a common complaint from sufferers nowadays is that the time has passed too slowly in hospital because they've had nothing to do. This seemed to be a waste of an opportunity to involve patients in social and practical activities (4). 'It seems to me that without this sort of provision, hospitals may – in some cases – still provide asylum, but nothing else, while doctors wait for the medication to work!' a carer summed up the general feeling.

A depressing environment?

Several members felt that the urinating on the floor – left for many hours – and the placing of a woman patient who habitually stripped when others were present in a corner of the dining-room which also doubled up as the room to meet up with visitors, were symptoms of a demoralized service where staff had come to believe they could achieve no better than this. 'Very much part of the culture which led Naomi to feel there was no optimism that people were expected to recover, isn't it?' one of them suggested. This was the general feeling and members wound up the analysis on this rather depressing note, quite able to identify with Naomi's assessment of her experience as 'detention without therapy'.

THE WIDER PERSPECTIVE

The group went on to discuss some of the concerns raised in their analysis of this case study.

A role for a mediator?

As has been noted, one member felt that Ron had needed someone to mediate for him when he could get no answers at all about his wife's illness and when he was worried about her being allowed to come and go from the hospital as she pleased. This was a service that the group felt could be invaluable for carers and it seemed to them that it could be provided – initially anyway – by voluntary workers with some knowledge or experience of the mental health services. They believed that it should suffice to have someone readily available for a few hours – perhaps a couple of times a week – and for the service to be well advertised within the hospital as well as, where available, in any introductory literature.

Duty to care revisited

When the LEAP group worked on cases featured in the first two books in this series they asked several times 'but what about a duty to care?' on the part of staff working with a sufferer. This came up again when they looked at this case study. There were several examples which they noted:

(a) Naomi felt threatened by several patients on the ward.

(b) When still manic, she had inappropriate feelings towards a male patient and bought him presents.

(c) When still manic, delusional and unaware of the dangers of passing traffic, she was allowed to go out in the nearby town on her own.

(d) In the evenings she was allowed to go out to the local pub with other patients.

Members felt that all of these situations needed addressing. They agreed that patients – and particularly first-time MD sufferers – need explanations about the way their illness can affect their feelings and perceptions if they are not to be put at risk of making inappropriate – and perhaps disastrous – relationships. They also need to be able to talk with staff about anything or anyone that scares them on the ward. In other words, patients need to be protected and to feel as safe as their illness allows and its up to the ward team to provide this security. 'And they also need protection from dangers outside the hospital too – like spending money recklessly, becoming involved with undesirable strangers and running the risk of causing a road accident', a carer nicely summed up the feeling of the group.

Finally, members insisted that someone still having psychotic symptoms and not yet stabilized on medication should not be allowed to accompany other patients to the local pub. 'All it takes is some time spent discussing this with the patient and, hopefully, the provision of some alternative form of entertainment or activity within the ward', a survivor suggested. This seemed a profoundly sensible way of focusing on the patient's right to care and protection rather than emphasizing their right to do as they wish!

Insisting on a 'duty to care'?

The LEAP group wondered how those closest to the patient should act if they had a similar experience to that of Naomi and Ron. There seemed to be little doubt that members would advise any families finding themselves in this position to record their concern – ie, by speaking to the member of staff in charge of the ward. 'And if this doesn't produce results, then put your complaint in writing, with a copy for the psychiatrist and for the hospital managers, as well as one for yourself!' a carer concluded.

Members were however very much aware of a general concern among carers about challenging the system – especially during the first episode of a serious mental illness – in case they caused problems for the patient and became known as a problem family! Whether or not such fears were justified was quite another matter because it seemed to be human nature to think this way about taking any action which might affect a loved one. 'Nevertheless, it's as well to weigh up the matter carefully and if the patient is definitely at risk, to do something about it – if only to ask for a copy of the hospital's policy on this matter. Things won't change otherwise, will they?' This member's contribution seemed to sum up the general feeling on this admittedly worrying problem. The group also felt that the sort of mediator they are recommending for every hospital would be in a good position to ask such questions on behalf of concerned relatives.

Unnecessary confusion?

Finally, members came back to the subject which seems to be frequently brought up by visiting staff and lay people entering a psychiatric ward; the problem of trying to work out who is in charge and, indeed, who are staff and who are patients! It seemed to the LEAP group that everyone is disadvantaged by the confusion which confronts them as they enter the ward. A survivor pointed out that first-time sufferers are often particularly confused by a system where patients and staff all look the same. 'This doesn't do anything to make them feel more secure', she added, 'and I believe it just feeds into the common delusion that one's fellow patients are in fact staff spying on you!'

A carer asked if anyone knew why it was originally decided that psychiatric nurses should not wear uniform? I mean, everyone seems happy for nurses in ordinary hospitals to be in uniform, don't they?' he asked. After a pause, a survivor volunteered the opinion that the idea had been to make everything more informal and friendly as well as to encourage the patients not to see themselves as patients. 'If so,' she went on, 'the powers that be have missed the point; patients only feel things are informal and friendly if the staff make it that way. It's more about attitudes than about dress, isn't it?' Yes, another carer agreed and spoke wistfully about the time when a sister in starched uniform would come bustling up to greet any visitors on the ward. A survivor exclaimed 'In other words, fetch back the men in the white coats!' but agreed amid laughter that if psychiatric nurses were to wear uniform again then *everyone* might be less confused.

'And this would make for improved security too', the carer who had been shown to the men's dormitory by a patient reminded us.

SUMMING UP

The group felt that this case study reflected a particularly frustrating experience of a first-time episode of a serious mental illness and that it also raised several concerns. They felt the most important of these involved important basic rights; the right to have a diagnosis and explanations to go with it, the right to proper care and protection, the right to have meaningful involvement with staff and the right to have appropriate stimulation while in hospital. They also noted that this case study demonstrated that there are times when carers need special support and that it should not prove difficult or expensive to provide a mediation service in all hospitals rather than, as is the case at present, just in a few.

INFORMATION

The following pieces of information are relevant to points brought up during the group's analysis and discussion which have been highlighted in the text:

(1) and (2) A duty to care and protect

Patients with a serious mental illness such as manic depression may lose their usual inhibitions and feel bound to spend their money recklessly and maybe to behave excessively out of character in other ways. They are in hospital because their judgement is impaired enough for them to need care and protection and they have the right to expect this from the team supervising their treatment. Clearly, part of such protection should include warning patients about the risks of drinking alcohol when high, let alone when on medication too, and protecting them from these risks.

(3) Nurse/patient interaction

For further information, see the report of this survey carried out by The Mental Health Act Commission, in collaboration with The Sainsbury Centre for Mental Health in *British Medical Journal* (1998) *317*, 1279–1283 (Richard Ford, Graham Duncan, Lesley Warner, Pollyanna Hardy and Matt Muijen).

(4) A lack of stimulation

As we saw in Chapter 1, an *Acute Problems* survey of the quality of care in acute psychiatric wards, carried out by the Sainsbury Centre for Mental Health between September 1996 and April 1997, involving 215 patients in nine acute psychiatric wards throughout England and Wales, found that most patients were bored during their stay and few if any were involved in planned programmes of social activity, with 40 per cent of all patients undertaking no social or recreational activity. A free briefing paper, or the full report at £9 plus 10 per cent p&p, can be obtained from The Sainsbury Centre for Mental Health, 134–138 Borough High Street, London SE1 1LB.

EXERCISE

In what ways would you have expected nurses to be involved with Naomi and her husband during her first week in hospital?

CHAPTER 4

One family's nightmare

Sometimes the concept of 'confidentiality' is taken beyond anything which seems reasonable or in the interests of patients. Equally worrying, it is a concept which can be used to completely exclude families and even alienate them from a loved one. Let us examine what happened to Joe's family when he became ill.

CASE STUDY

While waiting to go away to university, Joe involved himself in voluntary work in his local community and went on to display leadership qualities and an enthusiasm for working with children. Later, in the middle of his second year at university a hundred miles or so from home, Joe was first admitted to hospital. This was shortly after his 21st birthday. No-one informed his family that he was in hospital and when his parents made their weekly telephone call to him, Joe's friends told them that he was staying at various friends' houses over the next few weeks and, no, they didn't have a forwarding address or telephone number.

Eventually, a month or so after they had last spoken with him, Joe wrote to his parents saying he planned to take time off from his studies for the rest of the college year and that, meanwhile, he would stay with several of his college pals in the university town rather than return home. He added that he had been in hospital having treatment for a 'stress related breakdown'.

When his parents and two brothers paid Joe a visit shortly after this, they were horrified to find how much he had changed. He was edgy – even high – and, seemingly, on a short fuse. Having always been close to his mother, he now kept her, as well as the rest of the family, at a distance and would say nothing about what had happened to him; which hospital he had been in, how he felt now and whether or not he was receiving any medical treatment. He did, however, talk at length about new deep religious convictions and this again disturbed his family as this was an aspect of Joe that was completely new to them. It was as if a loved one had become a stranger! Before they left they learned that even his close friends 'trod with care'; they too weren't sure how to handle the new Joe. Indeed, they seemed to have no more information than the family did about what had happened and nor did the staff at his college.

This situation continued in much the same way during the next six months or so and the family felt as if they were stepping on ice whenever they were with Joe. Sometimes he was barely civil to them and they were quite sure that if they continued to ask questions about what had happened, he would refuse to have anything more to do with them. So nothing had been resolved by the time Joe returned to the university and, within a few weeks of doing so, he disappeared again. Once his parents realized it was all happening again, they immediately paid a visit to the college. As before, friends only knew that Joe had told them he was visiting friends for a few weeks and the college staff knew less than this; as far as they were concerned he had taken some 'leave'.

At this point, Joe's parents were seriously worried. One of their main fears was that he might have joined one of the extreme religious sects; they felt he was particularly vulnerable because he had become more and more preoccupied with religion and rarely talked about anything else. His mother fretted so much over the next few days that she made a return visit to the university town the following week, accompanied by a friend. The two women arranged bed and breakfast accommodation for themselves and, after some frantic detective work, they spent the next couple of days searching a fifteen-mile radius of hospitals and day centres and the like. After feeling instinctively that Joe was known at one clinic they had visited because of the embarrassed reaction they received, they returned there and this time the mother put pressure on the receptionist. Very reluctantly, she was told they knew Joe at the clinic and was given a telephone number and name of a psychiatrist. On calling this number, the mother found herself talking to a medical secretary and was asked to explain her interest in Joe. When she said he was her son, she was told to ring back in an hour. When she did this, the secretary then told her that the psychiatrist would not be speaking to, or seeing, her. She had left a message to the effect that Joe was a grown man now and suggested his mother go home and get on with her life. Furthermore, unless Joe signed a consent form, no information on him or his whereabouts could be relayed to the family. Dazed, the distressed woman put the receiver down, unable to speak. To this day, she doesn't know what was meant by a 'consent form' or whether Joe was asked to sign one.

Later, back home again, after talking with her husband and daughters, she sat down and wrote to the psychiatrist. Not knowing where the doctor worked, she sent the letter care of the clinic she visited, saying that it seemed to her that perhaps the doctor had a low opinion of her husband and herself as parents and blamed them for whatever it was that was happening to Joe? She begged the doctor to reconsider her decision not to meet the family. They all cared so much for Joe and all she asked was that the doctor should give them a little of her time so that she could make a more informed decision about them and the sort of people they were.

The mother never received a reply of any kind. Four years later, this woman still winces when she talks about the weeks which followed her conversation with the medical secretary. 'In fact', she says, 'we all felt bereaved; we felt we had lost Joe for ever. That was the worst time of all.'

It was to be another four weeks before her son was well enough to get around to 'phoning his family to tell them where he was. As it turned out, Joe had not even been aware of their concern about him nor about their efforts to find him.

During the rest of that year and the following one, Joe was in and out of hospital countless times. His mother eventually succeeded, after several days of negotiation, in arranging for her and Joe's elder brother to meet with the medical team to discuss his diagnosis and treatment. She was alarmed to be told that, as a result of her request, Joe had to be subjected to a full meeting with the hospital staff to see what might be discussed at a meeting with his family. In the event, mother and brother met with a junior doctor – not the psychiatrist – in Joe's presence and they were dismayed to find that the latter was so confused and ill that he was unaware of what was going on. Despite all their best efforts, they came away without having been given a diagnosis or clear answers to any of the questions they had carefully prepared. Neither did they receive a response to their request for advice as to how to help and support Joe. As it was, they were by this time paralyzed with fear that everything they did made things worse because they seemed quite unable to engage with him. They sensed that Joe felt threatened by them and they didn't know why, or what to do about this. They left the hospital none the wiser and even more distressed about his condition.

During the next eighteen months, the family gleaned the information – from Joe during times when he felt more well – that on some of his stays in hospital he had been given electrical treatment. They also gathered that he had taken to 'hurting himself', as his mother puts it. At worst, this manifested itself in attempts at suicide by overdosing. By now, he had also been admitted to hospital under the Mental Health Act several times. The family visited Joe whenever he was agreeable to this and he even came back home with them on the rare occasion, when he then retired to bed throughout his stay.

Sometimes Joe seemed to change and seemed more well and like his old self, particularly during the periods he was recovering from a relapse. However, he would then suddenly deteriorate again – this, it turned out later, was when the medication he was given at such times was reduced because it was considered to be too high a dose. The family did not know anything about this medication but when they asked on one occasion, 'largactil' was mentioned. When the mother asked around she was told that largactil was the original drug which was responsible for the breakthrough in the treatment of schizo-phrenia – the first of many similar drugs which were to be effective in controlling the bizarre symptoms typical of a psychotic breakdown. When she tentatively asked a junior doctor some weeks later if Joe suffered with schizophrenia, she received the shocked answer, 'Stress-related breakdown is our diagnosis. Some get over it, some learn to live with it and others don't. Only time will tell.' She could get no further with this conversation and gave up on it. Joe continued to be given courses of Electric Convulsive Therapy (ECT).

Things went on like this until one dreadful day the family learned from the hospital that Joe was on a life support machine after a particularly horrific attempt to end his life – this time on the ward – which was to leave him with permanent injuries. This incident was followed by weeks of pain and anguish for everyone involved. Things gradually improved over the next few months, with the family beginning to relax again, until Joe's mother received a phone call from someone from the hospital wanting to speak to her husband. She explained that he was at work and was not immediately available, asking nervously, 'Why, what has happened?' She was told, abruptly, that as her husband was older than her he was the 'nearest relative' and they couldn't give details to anyone else. Having just about come to terms with the horrors of the previous few months, Joe's mother felt faint with terror and begged to be told what had happened now; to no avail – she learned nothing further until she managed to contact her husband one and a half hours later and he rang the hospital. As it turned out, nothing untoward had happened and the mother had gone through this further anguish without any need. As she asked later, 'Why this obsession with confidentiality? Why couldn't they understand my need to know what was happening after everything we'd been through so recently?'

Joe is still in hospital, back once more on a voluntary basis, with his last stay having extended well over a year. However, there is talk of his being prepared for discharge to his flat soon. Although this should be good news, it is difficult for the family to relax each time they learn that Joe is to be discharged because it always seems to be an impossibly uphill struggle for him to settle 'out in the community' again. Predictably, his college friends all disappeared long ago and he is reliant on members of the family – living one hundred miles away – for social support. While he has up to now turned down any suggestion of returning home – and his mother has avoided putting any pressure on him about this – it has been quite clear in the past that Joe certainly welcomes phone calls and visits from the family at these times. Meanwhile, his parents have still never met the psychiatrist (even during the recent life and death crisis); requests to see her have been ignored in the same way that the mother's original letter was ignored. They are particularly concerned that Joe seems to have had no choice but to agree each time he is offered a course of ECT and his mother believes that they should have been given a chance to talk with his doctor, on their son's behalf, about what she feels is 'such an intrusive treatment on such a sensitive organ as the mind.' They cannot see how Joe can be considered fit to make decisions about such matters when he becomes really ill, nor to make decisions at such times about whether or not the family should be told anything. It is very clear that Joe gets in touch with them whenever he is well enough to cope with making a telephone call but when he is in the 'pit of hell', as his mother describes the worst phases of his illness, and his parents want to know what is happening, Joe has to meet with the staff team to decide if he wants them to share any information with his family and, if so, what this should be. Since they realized this, the family have been very reluctant to put this extra strain on him.

Despite the pain and despair of the past few years, it is noteworthy that Joe's family cannot fault the caring that he has received from some of the nursing staff he has had daily contact with and also from social workers who have helped to rehabilitate him in the community between relapses. As his mother puts it, 'This has been tender loving care – some of them have helped beyond the call of duty and we're grateful, to say the least.' It is also clear to them that Joe completely trusts the psychiatrist – is in fact very dependent upon her – and they are reluctant to 'rock the boat' and do anything which would worsen things for their son. They just wish they could be trusted and taken into the medical team's confidence so that they might have some peace of mind instead of constantly worrying that they may be failing to protect their son's best interests.

COMMENT

This case is a worrying example of the attitude of some mental health professionals towards carers, or, rather, would-be carers. If the reason for withholding information from this family is due to paranoia affecting Joe's judgement when he relapses, then it is a pity that this has not been explained to them, with all its implications. The team can hardly be unaware of the fact that their patient maintains contact with his family when he is more well. However, you may wish to consider whether there might be other explanations for the reticence of this psychiatrist and her team?

Perhaps it would be a good idea at this point to pause and go through the case study again, highlighting any points where you feel that the concept of confidentiality has been carried to extremes and even militated against the interests of the patient and/or his family?

GROUP'S ANALYSIS OF THE CASE STUDY

The LEAP Group has been frustrated by several cases it has worked on in the *Living with Serious Mental Illness* series where families have been ignored, even victimized, by service providers. The general feeling about this one was summed up by someone's comment, 'well, it fair takes your breath away'.

A responsibility to tell?

There was genuine amazement amongst members that a student could be admitted to hospital without the staff or managers having a responsibility to notify the university and, through them, the family. While no-one was sure whether or not this might be a legal obligation – as Joe was over 21 years at the time – members had no doubt that it amounted to madness not to inform anyone and, particularly, the nearest relative. 'If this was normal practice, then the Salvation Army would spend most of its time searching for missing persons!' exclaimed a bemused carer.

A 'consent form' and a 'briefing' meeting

The group had never heard of patients being asked to sign consent forms before their families could be informed of their whereabouts and other basic facts. It seemed to them that if this hospital did have such a procedure then it might act as a deterrent against depressed or paranoid patients keeping in touch with their relatives. To expect them to actually sign a form to this effect when they may be depressed, frightened or paranoid would seem to be the least likely way of achieving this aim.

Someone remarked that 'this reference to a "consent form" had the same feel about it as the rumpus which resulted from the mother's request to meet with Joe's doctors.' Members couldn't understand what that was all about either and agreed with the carer who observed that 'it seemed almost barbaric to expose Joe to a meeting with the whole team to discuss what could be said to his family at a time when he was clearly very unwell!'

'Yes,' exclaimed a survivor, 'it immediately brought back memories of ward rounds at times when I was psychotic. It used to feel like it was an inquisition. The last thing you need at times like that is a sea of faces all focusing on you, let alone taxing you with questions!' 'This seems to me to be another "deterrent" for the family. Whatever effect it had on Joe – and he certainly wasn't really well enough to take part in the meeting with his sister and mother shortly afterwards – it certainly put the family off suggesting more of the same, didn't it?' mused a second survivor. 'Yes, and all that hype, only to see a junior doctor in the presence of the patient anyway,' agreed a carer, 'and what was there to hide that Joe had to be there despite his having been subjected to a 'briefing' meeting beforehand? The whole thing seems really paranoid to me! You could be forgiven for wondering if this was a secret society rather than a hospital, couldn't you?'

The more members thought about it, the more mystified they became as to how all this secrecy and fuss could be justified in the name of 'confidentiality'. They decided to come back to this issue later.

An introduction to mental illness

The group could identify only too well with this family's dilemma when they eventually caught up with Joe after his first breakdown. 'When a serious mental illness isn't properly controlled, it can seem like someone you know and love has turned into an alien!' a carer sighed. 'And "stepping on ice" just about sums up the feeling, doesn't it?' Yes, others had been there too, 'but not in complete ignorance about mental illness', pointed out a carer. 'That was so unfair; his family needed to know but they could see it was winding Joe up to ask him questions. What were they meant to do, for goodness sake?'

'Yes,' another member agreed, 'and that's exactly how it is for me when my son's ill – he gets very tetchy if you persist in questioning him. I know exactly how Joe's family must have felt, not even knowing anything about mental illness'. She paused for a moment before adding, 'I guess they'd never heard of paranoia and that this was probably the reason for his hostility'. 'Well, yes,' agreed a survivor, 'and I don't see how this could be helpful to Joe. The family needed to know about crucial things like that (1) and they needed to be able to ask someone about his sudden preoccupation with religion too. Apparently, this got worse later on – it could have been a sign of psychotic illness but it could also have meant Joe had got involved with an extremist group as the mother feared. I feel for her; I can't see what she was meant to do!'

A lack of compassion

'Well, she didn't get much further when she eventually tracked down the psychiatrist after Joe became ill again, did she?' a second survivor pointed out, 'how could she be so heartless as to tell this woman to go away and get on with her life? Her son is part of her life!'

Members found this very worrying; not only was this a chilling response to the mother's attempts to find her son, it also seemed that the psychiatrist was prepared to 'play God', as someone put it, and decide it was better for her patient if she turned his family away. 'How could she do this,' a carer asked, 'even if Joe was paranoid about his mother at this time – and goodness knows a psychiatrist should understand this – how could she take the attitude he was better off without his family. Who was meant to take their place?'

'Quite!' exclaimed another. 'As one would expect, all Joe's college friends have gone long ago. This is one of the reasons why sufferers need their families and why those who lose them can be so isolated and vulnerable. How could this doctor as good as invite Joe's to turn their backs on him?'

The group found this all very disturbing. Not only had this family been kept in ignorance about Joe's first episode of a serious mental illness and left to cope as best they could over the following months, then the psychiatrist turned them away when he'd relapsed without any information at all except, it seemed, a pointed invitation to forget Joe. This seemed to them to go beyond even an exaggerated pre-occupation with confidentiality.

Indeed, a survivor pointed out that the mother's letter to the psychiatrist following this unfortunate incident asked nothing more than a meeting with the family and a proper opportunity for her to decide for herself if they really cared for Joe and what sort of people they were, adding, 'She was not asking to discuss Joe and therefore no confidentiality was being breached.'

A bereavement

Members felt very keenly the mother's desperation after being turned away like this and could quite understand why she says the family felt bereaved, like they had lost Joe for ever. One survivor commented, 'Yes, I remember my husband saying it was as though I had died. Without information, this is a natural reaction.' 'And, they could have been quite right about feeling they had lost Joe, couldn't they?' a mother pointed out, 'They may have felt the psychiatrist was virtually saying that he had finished with them. It certainly must have seemed that way to the family.' 'And it's seriously worrying to discover that Joe knew nothing about their concern, so it seems that no-one had put this to him or let him know that his family had been asking about him. If this is the case, then surely this is contravening the patient's rights?' another member suggested. 'Anyway, I think it is. I'd have been very angry if this had happened to me when I was in hospital. And leaving him in ignorance of his family's concern could hardly have done anything for his morale or helped him to gradually sort things out if he was paranoid at the time!'

A family trying to make sense of it all

Despite the fact that Joe's illness seemed to escalate over the following couple of years, members were encouraged to note that he was prepared to go home occasionally. However, a carer pointed out that he immediately retired to bed. 'And I don't suppose his poor mother knew what to do about that. I've been there with my son and I found it such a relief to talk with one of the nurses after it had happened a couple of times and to have her advise me to insist that he come downstairs for a couple of hours at a time, if only to eat a meal. It worked when I realized that I was helping him by doing this and we gradually saw more of him each visit. I suppose Joe's mother would be scared of upsetting him and I can identify with that.' she added with feeling. 'Yes,' agreed a survivor, 'this makes me cross. They have not been given any opportunity to cope and to support Joe effectively. How can his doctor believe she's doing her patient any favours?'

The group was interested to note that Joe seemed much more well and like his old self when he was recovering from a relapse and that it turned out that at those times he was probably taking largactil. Could it be that the rest of the time he was being treated for the wrong illness? It certainly seemed possible if taking this medicine made such a change in him when he should have been very vulnerable. Why couldn't this achievement have been sustained? Furthermore, several challenged the concept of 'too high a dose' in this context.

A survivor asked, 'If the dose was too high, why was Joe on it in the first place?' and another asked, 'why was he doing well on it if the dose was too high?' and, similarly, a carer wanted to know, 'why was the medication constantly reduced when he always deteriorated at that point?'

Another matter which concerned some members was the matter of Joe having ECT; quite frequently, they gathered. They could identify with the parents' concern and they also wondered if it was achieving anything for Joe. Also, did this treatment account for a couple of comments about his not being able to remember things a lot of the time? Did the use of ECT mean that Joe didn't have schizophrenia or a similar illness, others wanted to know? If so, why did largactil seem to have such a positive effect on him? Yes, the group had lots of questions to ask, but no answers. 'Rather like Joe's family, I suppose', observed a carer with a rueful grin.

Accolade

At this point, members decided there was little more to be achieved by pursuing this analysis, but paused before moving on to note with pleasure that there was some really encouraging news at the end of the case study with Joe's mother expressing her gratitude for the 'tender loving care' that Joe had received throughout from some of the nursing staff and local social workers. Not only was this splendid news but the group felt that such a generous comment by a mother who had been excluded from any meaningful information about her son's condition, care and treatment suggested that a little more sharing with this family might have proved to be a very positive move for everyone concerned.

THE WIDER PERSPECTIVE

As might be suspected, the group's main concern in this case was the way this family were treated and what members saw as the abuse of the concept of confidentiality to keep them at bay.

A neglected resource

'It's such a waste really, isn't it?' grumbled a carer, 'that the team working with Joe have never had the benefit of learning about the family's experience of him before he was ill?'

'Well, yes,' agreed a survivor, 'and it makes you wonder what sort of assessment can be made of patients by teams who have no real knowledge of their past, doesn't it?' After a pause, she added, 'I wonder if things might have gone differently for Joe if the psychiatrist had found out more about his past?' 'And that isn't all the family could offer, is it?'

complained another survivor, 'This family haven't been given the chance to understand the sort of experiences he has and how he might be feeling about them and about his illness generally. They could be an important source of strength for him if only his doctor understood this.' 'Yes, and goodness knows they want to help!' someone exclaimed, 'There's nothing worse than standing on the sidelines twiddling your thumbs; frightened to intervene!'

Several members wondered if the parents really should have intervened and gone above the doctor, insisting on a better service but others pointed out that families were often very backward in coming forward. 'I think the mother sums it up well when she says they've been scared of spoiling things for Joe – we shouldn't forget that he was clearly dependent upon this psychiatrist by the time they caught up with him again!' one of them exclaimed. 'Yes, it's true that they could have gone "above her" about the principle of keeping them in the dark from the start but what would that achieved if it had really alienated Joe from the family once and for all? At least they are still in there, aren't they?' another pointed out. 'Well, yes, and so they should be! Joe needs them and it's no thanks to this doctor that they are still in there.' A survivor was troubled about this, 'I don't understand why families can be excluded in this way.'

Confidentiality?

At this point, members focused once more on the vexing question of why indeed Joe's family had been treated this way. On reflection they didn't feel that all, or even most, of the instances which had been quoted could be put down to the concept of confidentiality. As someone had already pointed out, there was no need for the psychiatrist to ignore the mother's letter or to decline to meet with the family on the grounds of confidentiality. A survivor was concerned about the 'confidentiality' concept and how frequently this subject comes up:

> 'It's used to excuse everything and given as a reason not to tell anyone anything,' she pointed out, adding 'What we need is a sensible definition of this so-called "confidentiality", don't we?' (2) No-one, it seemed, could argue with that!

Fostering over-dependence?

One survivor in the group was not at all happy about the 'trusting and dependent relationship' that Joe seemingly had with his psychiatrist. She reminded us of the 'clinging relationships' that were commonly formed in schizophrenia, for example, and the need to try and avoid this type of dependency if at all possible (3). A carer agreed and said she would be happier about this trusting relationship if the doctor had sought a second opinion when her patient was clearly making no progress. As it was, Joe was really bound to take whatever advice was offered and to agree to whatever treatment was offered and this would have been even more of a problem in her eyes if the family had not been determined to 'stay in there'. A second survivor nodded, saying, with a smile, 'Well, we've found another good reason for backing families.'

A reliance on outdated theories?

At this point, the LEAP Group rather reluctantly returned to a theme which seemed to crop up a little too frequently when they analyse case studies where things don't go too well for sufferers and their families; the clinging of some professionals to theories discredited in the 1970s that families cause serious mental illness in their relatives (4). It did seem possible that this psychiatrist and her team might well blame Joe's family for his illness (as the mother had instinctively suggested in the letter she wrote to the doctor after being turned away on the telephone); this could explain, but not excuse, the complete exclusion of the parents from the start. Moreover, it was the only explanation that the group could find for the psychiatrist taking it upon herself to try and discourage the family from keeping in touch with her patient. It only made any sense to them if she was misguided enough to still be influenced by out-of-date and officially discredited theories. However, as members agreed, this was yet another query about this particular case study for which they had no answer. This seemed to be the price to be paid for the putting up of a 'smoke screen' rather than the generating of openness and communication and a sharing of resources.

SUMMING UP

This perplexing and disturbing case seems to have raised a lot of issues, all of which seem to originate from a desire to treat the patient within a vacuum, ignoring both his past and those involved in it. By doing this, members of his family have been rendered impotent and not knowing how to help, with no role other than their determination to be there for their relative, come what may.

Again and again during their analysis and wider discussion, group members have asked, 'Don't families have any rights?' and, although it seems they must have, the LEAP group could nevertheless find no evidence of this being so in this case study.

INFORMATION

The following pieces of information are relevant to points brought up during the group's analysis and discussion which have been highlighted in the text:

(1) A local carers' group survey

This small, unpublished survey involved 21 out of a possible 22 families and they judged the following nine services to be a priority *at the time of a first episode* of a serious mental illness:

(i)   Support for the family

(ii)   Explanations about the illness

(iii)   Explanations about the way that symptoms may affect the sufferer

(iv)   Explanations about the role of medication and any side effects

(v)   The potential risks of further breakdown

(vi)   The providing of a 'lifeline' – what to do if needing help in the future

(vii) Advice about the benefits system and other practical services

(viii) Introduction to self-help organizations and relevant literature

(ix)   Information for *the sufferer* about the illness and how to cope.

(Cooper, S. and Howe, G. (1993) reported in Howe, G. (1994) *Working with Schizophrenia*. London: Jessica Kingsley Publishers, 44–45, 73–76.)

(2) Confidentiality

The concept of medical confidentiality is well known to most of us. In the context we are discussing here, references to 'confidentiality' relate to the fact that the Mental Health Act 1983 allows for patients, once 18 years of age, to request that details of their illness and treatment are withheld from others, including their families. Whereas such a stipulation might not cause too many problems in general medicine, this is not the case in psychiatry when many patients suffer with a serious mental illness such as schizophrenia which can involve paranoia about loved ones, ie those who matter most, at times of breakdown. At such times, patients may take advantage of this right and, unless mental health workers intervene and mediate, then families can be left in ignorance about the illness while being expected to support and care for the patient out in the community. Not only can it be argued that this bizarre situation amounts to abuse of those who support and care for a patient with a serious mental illness, but it also renders them unable to do this effectively.

Despite encouragement from two successive governments for carers to be included in planning for the patient's future, some professionals seem content to exclude families as we have seen in this chapter. See Chapter 7 (p.109) for an example of how this can work out in practice.

(3) A risk of over-dependency

During the worst times of a serious mental illness, and schizophrenia in particular, there is a tendency for sufferers to become very dependent on one other person. This is more often than not the mother or another close relative but sometimes it may be a formal carer such as a nurse or social worker. This can become an intense and 'clinging' and exclusive relationship, shutting out even other family members living in the same household. In effect, the relationship becomes a 'lifeline' for a sufferer shunning everyone and everything else until better health returns. It is this which makes it helpful for several members of staff, rather than one, to be involved with the patient from the start of a stay in hospital, to avoid any such dependency developing and to open up opportunities for gradually making other social contacts.

(4) The family theories

During the 1960s and 1970s there was an abundance of theories of a similar kind which blamed the families of schizophrenia sufferers for their relative's illness. These popular ideas dominated much of the literature and received wisdom of the time and added significantly to the misery of families trying to cope with living with a serious mental illness. Long since discredited and abandoned because, among other things, researchers were discovering for the first time the idiosyncrasies of normal family life rather than anything unusual about families coping with schizophrenia, they have nevertheless influenced for many years the attitudes of some of those who in turn have influence over the training and supervision of recruits to the caring professions; those interested in this phenomenon might like to read Christine Heron's chapter on mental health carers in *Working with Carers*, (1998). London: Jessica Kingsley Publishers.

For a full discussion and useful references on the family theories, see Gwen Howe (1991) *The Reality of Schizophrenia*. London: Faber & Faber, pp.79–81.

EXERCISE

In this chapter, a survivor is quoted as saying that 'confidentiality is used to excuse everything and given as a reason not to tell anyone anything.'

Please comment in the light of (a) this team's lack of communication with their patient's family and (b) the sort of services which were highlighted as priorities by members of a carers' group in the above survey.

CHAPTER 5

Two very different experiences

Sometimes sufferers report that they have been well treated and cared for on one admission to hospital and have been accused of being difficult and attention-seeking on another. It was like this for Sue and she describes here what happened to her.

CASE STUDY – PART 1

A positive experience

'I had my first schizophrenic breakdown in the mid-1980s just about the time I should have been preparing to go to college. I had been miserably unwell for some time before that. I liked the psychiatrist who had been treating me for depression for the previous few months and I suspect that is why I agreed to go into hospital when he asked me. I didn't tell him what was really happening to me – I took it for granted that everyone must know I was going to die because I had done something dreadful. I just wished I knew what I was meant to have done! In the end it was my mother who told the doctor how paranoid I had become about the rest of the family and that I believed that they and our neighbours were planning to kill me.

'When I had been shown round the ward, a friendly nurse brought me a cup of tea and a sandwich, saying, 'it's a long time till lunchtime and you haven't eaten for some time.' She told me that everything was going to be alright and I wasn't to worry about the voices. I'd no idea what she was talking about but nodded because she seemed kind and concerned. She often came up and talked with me during the weeks that followed.

'Someone else who came to see me on that first day was an occupational therapist – or OT for short, she explained. She asked me about my hobbies; what interested me and how I usually spent my spare time? I told her I used to like to play music and racquet games and was good at sewing. I was also learning to type. That was a speech for me at that time but she seemed to want to know and talking about it made me believe just for a moment that everything was still like it used to be. Next day, another OT brought me a sewing kit and some material. We explored this together and sorted out something I could make during my first few days in hospital.

'Later in the week, after lying awake at night listening to our neighbours at home talking about me and how I was going to die, I became desperate enough to make two attempts at doing just that as I couldn't bear listening to their voices going on and on. The first time, a nurse caught up with me just as I stepped into the busy road outside and I can still hear the screeching of brakes all around us. The second time, I innocently asked if I could go and make myself a cup of tea one evening and another nurse caught me hiding a bread knife under my dressing-gown. I was never allowed to make myself a cup of tea after that without a member of staff or one of my fellow patients coming with me! That night, a nurse gave me an injection – to help me get some sleep, he told me. To put me to sleep, you mean, I thought … And again, I nodded; this was it – my waiting was over and somehow it didn't matter any more. I was surprised to wake up next morning and the next and the next! Before long, I begun to wonder if I wasn't meant to die, particularly as I had stopped hearing family and neighbours talking about me at night. I hadn't realized at that point how incongruous it was that I could hear their voices on the ward in the middle of the night – the hospital was miles away from our home.

'About that time the nurse who had welcomed me to the ward suggested she and I should go and have a look at the occupational therapy department. I was not keen but when we arrived the OT who had spent so much time with me on my first day in hospital came up immediately with a big smile and suggested I stay for a while. She urged me to try some painting and I did, with some trepidation. The next day she asked me if I would like to practise my typing – if so I could use the old typewriter for an hour or so each day. I jumped at this and sometimes, tucked away in a quiet corner, I actually enjoyed myself. I found I could still type after all – the last time I had tried, my brain and my fingers seemed to have lost contact and I'd given up the struggle. Other good things happened too. One day when I couldn't seem to find anything to do, the OT asked if I would like to do some sculpture with clay? Well, yes, but I didn't know how. That didn't matter; we spent the next two hours together playing with the clay and making tiny animals. Later, this was something else which I became absorbed in and I soon graduated to making more sophisticated figures.

'As my confidence grew, a doctor, who didn't seem much older than me, persuaded me to talk about the sort of things that had been happening to me during the past months. I was hesitant at first – frightened he would think me quite mad if I talked about this but he was very reassuring and asked me lots of questions. Later, I told him everything and he assured me that things would soon be back to normal. I wanted to believe him and I agreed to have a second injection. I now know that first injection had already helped me and the doctors knew they were on the right track.

'Three of the nurses, including the one who had welcomed me onto the ward, spent time with me regularly. The male nurse who had given me the first injection and who was sometimes in charge of the ward, always came up to me and asked how I was getting on and what had I been doing the previous day? Once he asked me if I'd like to accompany him to a meeting of the hospital drama group – hospital staff and patients were making initial plans for a pantomime they would present at Christmas. I enjoyed this and became quite absorbed in all that was going around me. This wasn't what I'd imagined hospital would be like!

'I couldn't help noticing that the staff always included any patients nearby in their conversations. This helped to make me feel we all mattered and it helped me get to know everyone too; I would never have approached anyone on my own. The third nurse who was particularly friendly to me approached me one morning, all smiles, and said, 'shall you and I go and do some cooking?' and off we went to a kitchen allocated for this purpose and prepared a very passable meal. I remember I was quite clumsy and kept dropping things but I couldn't help but enjoy myself – the nurse made everything such fun – and I found something of an appetite for the first time for ages when we sat down to eat the results of our work.

'I remember other things about that first time in hospital. The ward staff treated my mother as if she mattered and I was so pleased about that. They always made her feel welcome and I found out later that whenever he was on duty the male nurse who got to know me well would have a word with her to let her know how I was getting on. I also realized later that he and his colleagues listened intently to anything she had to say about me, particularly when I was first admitted, because they knew all sorts of things about me which helped them make life easier when I was confused, scared and not very forthcoming.

'I left hospital feeling more confident than I had for a very long time. The OT who had helped me so much walked back to the ward with me on my last full day in the hospital and told me she knew I had withdrawn from my friends and all my hobbies and she wanted me to start living life to the full again now. Could I do that? I told her that I thought I could and I remember going on to say that I thought other patients in the ward would get better too because they would realize they *mattered* and because of this they would stop believing they had done something dreadful the same way that I did. She looked rather thoughtful before giving me a big smile and wishing me lots of luck in the future.'

PART 2

A negative experience

Sue takes up her story twelve years later.

'My earlier attempts to give up taking medication had failed but twelve years after my breakdown I felt that I had been so well for so long that I decided it was time to get on with the rest of my life and to wean myself off the medication once and for all. After talking with my husband and a psychiatrist about it, I decided to do just that but unfortunately, six months later, I realized that everything was starting to go wrong again. Very scared, I asked my GP for help and he immediately put me back on my original medication. However, it turned out that the drug I had taken for so long no longer worked for me. A month later, I was very, very paranoid and I ran away from my husband because I was sure he was trying to poison me. I moved in with several friends in turn but left quickly because they each started to show the same sort of sinister designs on me. Some time later, I was sectioned and admitted to our local mental hospital; two counties away from the one where I was treated for my first breakdown.

'I was lucky with the psychiatrist who admitted me to hospital and he set about trying to find a drug which would help me back to good health. However, nothing else about this experience bore any resemblance to my first breakdown apart from the fact I again believed I must have done something horrendous but this time it was me versus the rest of the world! This time I had no allies. I believed that my mother and the rest of my family had succumbed to my husband's charms and would do whatever he told them. I made it clear they were not to visit me – I was really on my own now! Perhaps this was why I presented in a quite different way to when I broke down the first time and had been timid and accepting. I am told that the second time round I became quite demanding, even domineering, in my attempts to survive in a world which was now completely hostile towards me. What didn't show, it seems, is that I was more scared than I had ever been in my life.

'The biggest difference between this hospital and the first one was the nurses' attitude towards me. After the first day when I rushed around trying to make everyone understand what was happening to me and telling them I didn't want to die, they made it quite clear that they were "not going to reward this sort of behaviour". Quite simply, they thought I was just being difficult. They went on to act as if I wasn't there and it seems to me that this was made easier for them because I had a side room a little way along the corridor from their office. The ward team's apparent disdain and dislike of me only served to reinforce my own fears that I had done something really dreadful. Why else would they treat me this way? This was all the more painful for me because I was having to manage without any effective medication at this stage and was more and more aware of my husband and family plotting my death. Their voices were deafening, especially at night.

'I had nothing to do but sit around on the ward most of the time. I kept asking for something to do, anything at all, but to no avail. Eventually, I said I like to sew – could I do some sewing? Several days later – after repeated requests – I was given a few large pieces of old material and told I could do something with that if I wanted to. However, I was refused scissors. Apparently someone believed I was a suicide risk despite the fact that ward staff told me I was just behaving badly! As it seemed that no-one was prepared to spend a little time sitting with me so that I could use a pair of scissors and do something with these large pieces of material, nothing came of that venture. I still had nothing to do and felt totally isolated; my frustration and feelings of persecution worsened.

'The night nurses were different. Two of them would come and talk with me during my sleepless nights. One brought me a cup of tea in the early hours when she heard me crying. Their concern and kindness stand out as the only positive thing I remember about the staff during those dreadful weeks. Even the junior doctor who came on the ward most days seemed to have no time for me and gave me the impression there were more deserving and less well patients than me that he needed to attend to. He may well have felt he couldn't do anything for me until some effective medication was prescribed but, looking back, a few words of kindness and sympathy would have gone a long way.

'At last I was prescribed medication which calmed my worst fears. The overwhelming feelings of dread and restlessness went away almost immediately and my delusional ideas gradually faded during the following two weeks. The attitude of the ward staff changed almost immediately. One of the nurses came up to me before I went home to say 'do keep taking the medication, Sue, because it obviously suits you and it has helped you in a very short time.' She seemed really surprised and I believe – and so does my husband – that she was the only nurse to make the connection with the medication. Another nurse came up to me apologetically when I left to say 'but we didn't know what to do with you!' Apart from these two, none of the nurses made any comment at all but it seemed they now found me deserving of their time. They were now friendly and even started to give me the respect I had so craved when I was ill.

'Looking back, it would seem that the ward team took little notice of my family and various friends who had persevered throughout the weeks before I started to get well, trying to make them understand that this wasn't the Sue they knew. They even continued to ignore my husband completely when at last I was prepared to have him visit me. He spent most of his time at the hospital after that and the nurses acted as if he wasn't there – they were very good at doing that! It seems they had believed my previous protests that he was trying to poison me and they now continued to do so although there wasn't a scrap of evidence to back this up. His obvious concern for my welfare did nothing to change their attitude.

'Just before I was discharged, I discovered that I had been on 'close observation' at one point. When I queried this, we learned that nurses took it in turns to sit where they could watch the door of my room. To think that this was during the time when I felt so isolated and alone in a dangerous world that I kept pleading for help!

'I suspect that the staff would have a different perspective to mine about all this. My paranoia was such that I may well have seemed hostile and demanding. It might have been easier for them to decide I was just being difficult and ignore me but why, if that was the case, did two night nurses make a fuss of me? Although two of the nurses in the day team were concerned enough to acknowledge before I left that they now realized I'd been ill, no-one made an opportunity to talk through with me my frustration about the way I had been treated during my stay there or to ask me how it had been for me. Two years later, I still have flashbacks about this second admission to hospital and they continue to upset me.'

COMMENT

Sue's experiences may be unusual only in the sense that what happened to her during her two breakdowns seems to have reflected the opposite ends of the continuum as far as the care element of hospital treatment and care is concerned.

You might consider it worthwhile at this stage to pause for a moment and consider what might have contributed to these dramatically opposed approaches of handling a serious mental illness and how you feel about this.

GROUP'S ANALYSIS OF CASE STUDY

It is not surprising that members of the LEAP group were startled that Sue could have had such an exceptionally good experience during her first admission to hospital and such a destructive one the second time round. In view of the startling differences in approach and standards of care, it seemed the best way to go about analysing this case study would be to compare each of the variables which might give some indication as to why she should have been subjected to two such very different experiences.

The psychiatrists

It seemed quite clear to the group that Sue had no complaints of any kind about either of the psychiatrists who had admitted her to hospital. 'There's no mistaking the fact that Sue thinks highly of both these doctors', a survivor observed. 'Yes – it seems that this extraordinary difference in the standards of care she received was probably not influenced by them,' a carer agreed, 'but that seems rather odd to me'.

'Well, yes, but we don't really know whether or not both of these doctors were happy with their ward teams, do we?' suggested a second survivor. 'While some psychiatrists seem all-powerful – to the likes of us, anyway – others probably don't like to throw their weight around', she added.

'I'd go further than that', a second carer joined in. 'I know at least one psychiatrist who acts as if he is intimidated by colleagues from other disciplines. He seems to spend his time demonstrating that he is embarrassed by the old "medical model" of serious mental illness even though he insists that medication is an essential part of its treatment.' 'And, if that's the case,' someone concluded, 'then we'd never know whether the second doctor realized the level of care which Sue was receiving, let alone whether or not he could have influenced this.'

The hospital environment

The group noted that there seemed to be some good features in the first hospital such as tea-making facilities for the patients in the ward and a kitchen put aside for cooking sessions. They had no way of knowing whether any such arrangements were available at the second hospital, and, if so, whether or not they were taken advantage of. One important difference was the apparent lack of an occupational therapy department in the second hospital but, as someone pointed out, 'that's not so unusual in the 1990s is it? The OTs seem to be out in the community now.' 'Yes, a few of them do still work in the hospitals as well, but not many', a carer agreed.

A survivor pointed out that where there is no OT involvement, this can make life more difficult for nurses on the ward as their staffing arrangements have always been based on the premise that most of the patients would be away from the ward for at least several hours during each weekday. It was not unusual to find that nothing has replaced this facility. 'This might explain the lack of stimulation of any kind in the second ward and lack of any initiative by the nurses to provide any.'

This brought members to the next variable they wanted to consider.

The nursing staff

They felt that the welcome Sue received on the first ward was warming, to say the least. 'And', someone said, 'the nurse let her know that everything would be open and above board by as good as saying that they knew she hadn't been eating properly. I liked that.'

The group was most impressed by the sufferer's account of her interaction with the nurses. 'It looks as if several nurses attached themselves to each patient, doesn't it?' suggested a carer, 'And that not only avoids the building up of too much dependency with one member of staff (1) but it means that the sufferer gets to know and relate to more individuals which is good "social therapy", isn't it?'

Yes, other members thought this was an ideal arrangement and that it seemed to be handled so thoughtfully by the nurses concerned that Sue begun to realize that she and her fellow patients mattered. 'I like the way the nurses involved her in things outside the ward as well,' a second carer enthused, 'taking her to see the drama group in action and for a special one-to-one cooking session seem such happy, normal things to do!'

'And what about the nurses in the second hospital?' exclaimed a carer. 'I accept the point that there may have been more pressures on them because of the absence of OT staff but can anyone find any other reasons for their apparent lack of basic caring?' 'Well, only that she presented in a very different way the first time to the second time round. And we can assume that the second ward team would have been much happier with the Sue that the first ward team looked after!' offered a survivor with a wry smile.

'Yes and that does raise the query 'how well would the first ward team have coped if Sue had been admitted to the first hospital again when she had her second breakdown?' a second carer agreed. 'Well, we'll never know now, will we? But I suspect their system of allocating several nurses to each patient would have helped to meet Sue's need to talk with someone frequently. There seems to have been no attempt to relate to individual patients in this way in the second ward. Not one single nurse seems to have had any responsibility for Sue!' someone pointed out. 'That's right and if she really did run around all day begging for help when she first arrived, then it would seem intelligent to have promised her a certain amount of time each day with one or two members of staff – to have structured the help offered rather than withdraw it!' insisted a survivor.

'Well, yes and if they had been really hard-pressed – and I tend to believe that wasn't the case as staff had time to be friendly when she was more well later – why didn't they help themselves and Sue by spending a half-an-hour with her every so often so that she could then get on and help herself? The need for someone to sit with her while she used the scissors was as a good example of this', a carer pointed out.

'Well, that's right – if nurses had time to sit and stare at the door of her room, then presumably they could have used some of that time to be with her, albeit for short periods, couldn't they?' someone suggested.

It seemed to the group that the ward team had decided that Sue was 'difficult' and that any efforts they made on her first day to placate her had failed to calm her down. Two survivors in the group voiced the opinion that professionals did not appreciate that when someone is really psychotic they need reassurance again and again. They felt it was likely that the nurses had found that any attempts to reassure Sue on her first day had resulted in what they might well see as 'more demands for attention'.

'It's quite worrying, really, when you think about it', a carer observed. 'It seems that with this approach the most severely ill patients will be given the least help because they are the ones whose behaviour is most likely to be seen as "attention seeking" or troublesome.' The group felt that was very sad. They also felt confident that this approach was destined to escalate Sue's distress and one consequence of this was to alienate her more than ever. In contrast, Sue clearly still appreciates the concern shown her by the two night nurses and their approach seemed to be much closer to that of the first ward team.

OT Staff

Members were very much inclined to believe that the complete absence of any member of OT staff to work with Sue during her second stay in hospital was extremely important in that it deprived her of an opportunity to stop dwelling on her paranoid thoughts and terrors.

'And it also deprived her of any chance of being assessed by someone outside the ward culture', a survivor pointed out. 'One of the very nice things about OTs in my experience', she went on, 'is that they don't come over as judgemental – they seem to distance themselves from such matters and just relate to the individual. Maybe I've been lucky, I don't know.'

'I suspect you are right', a carer joined in. 'As you know, my son's been in hospital for some time now and he tells us that the OT who works with him doesn't criticize him. The way he says it, I suspect he feels that everyone else tends to do just that!'

Members took a second look at the role of the OT who worked so closely with Sue in the first hospital. 'It seems to me that this woman played a key role in Sue's recovery,' one commented, 'and she was there from the start, visiting her on the first day and arranging for her colleague to go back to the ward the next day to get the patient started on some sewing. This way, the OTs were very much part of the ward team as well as making a bridge with the community outside the ward'. 'Yes, preparing the patient for her first visit to the OT department where she clearly settled down quickly and happily,' added another, 'and that's where Sue was first able to pick up the threads of her old life and to start looking forward again.' 'Well, that's how I've always seen the role of the OT', a survivor, who rues the day that the old OT departments closed down, reminded us 'And I wish it could go on being like that. I used to find the staff so encouraging – their enthusiasm was irresistible. Now, they just seem to be running groups like everyone else!' She was not impressed!

Yes, even if a modernized, latter-day version of the OT department is out of the question, members wished that OTs could be in and out of wards to provide stimulation for the likes of Sue and other patients who complain of having nothing to do while in hospital (2). 'Coming back to this particular OT, I liked the way she walked back to the ward with Sue on her last day there – it sort of rounded off her stay there and she then helped Sue on her way with the "getting on with your life again" routine – it was all so positive and reassuring', was one survivor's opinion. 'Yes, rather different to Sue's memories of the second hospital', exclaimed another. 'Because no-one gave her an opportunity to talk through with them what had happened before the medication helped her, she is left with these flashbacks she talks about and they can't be good for her, can they?' No, the group agreed that this was an unhealthy legacy of a very unhappy experience.

Treatment of the family

On a happier note, members were encouraged to hear about the first ward team's treatment of Sue's mother and also noted how much this had pleased the sufferer! 'Really, this was an excellent example of the approach we have always advocated – communication both ways between formal and informal carers', exclaimed a carer. 'Yes, wasn't it?' someone agreed. 'First of all, the psychiatrist was able to admit Sue while she was still prepared to accept help because he took note of the mother's report that she was becoming really paranoid. Later, ward staff made a point of making sure that she and they shared any important information about the patient. It all helped to make Sue more secure, didn't it?'

'And what about the ward staff's attitude to family the second time round? If they had taken any notice of what they and Sue's friends were saying, then perhaps she would have been treated with love and care instead of scorn!' grumbled a carer. 'Yes, but the ward team's attitude towards the husband is very telling, isn't it? It seems to me that relatives and friends don't count at all with this team – they're not worthy of their consideration apparently', another carer observed.

'Well, that's right, isn't it?' a survivor agreed, 'and it might explain why they didn't seem to have any idea as to how to handle Sue's psychosis – it does help to know how the patient usually behaves and relates to people and they clearly didn't.' The analysis of this case study wound up at this point with the LEAP group still marvelling at the contrast between Sue's two experiences of being in hospital.

THE WIDER PERSPECTIVE

The LEAP group felt that the area of most obvious concern raised by this case study was the clear demonstration of the lack of any standardization in the quality of care and therapy offered to patients with a serious mental illness. Bearing in mind the legacy of the 1960s and 1970s when the medical model was rubbished and professional rivalry came into its own (see **THE WIDER PERSPECTIVE** in Chapter 2, p.32), members could not see how things would suddenly miraculously change in this direction. Meanwhile, one carer was very concerned about what seemed to be happening in the wards in which staff were evidently judgemental about their patients. 'What worries me about all this', she insisted, 'is that if they are not very careful those who work with a serious mental illness will come to believe that sufferers are inadequate and badly behaved – inferior to themselves in other words – instead of being plucky and determined survivors.'

One such survivor responded with a big grin, 'thank you, yes! I certainly don't feel there's any place for staff in hospitals to feel they have the right to judge me. In fact, I find I tend to look down on those who continue to work with serious mental illness without learning anything about it. I think they owe it to all of us to appreciate what happens when we become psychotic. Is that being unfair?' 'No, that seems to be an eminently reasonable reaction', a second carer responded promptly, 'but I sometimes feel we're whistling into the wind. How can we stop this decline of expertise?'

This question brought members back to a subject which has concerned them throughout this series; the apparent lack of any feedback for mental health workers on the outcome of a case they have been involved with at some point.

Lack of feedback and acceptance of a poor outcome

The group were particularly concerned that professionals involved in unhappy cases such as Julie's, Naomi's and Sue's, at the time of her second breakdown, should be given an opportunity to learn from the experience. They doubted, however, that there was much chance of this. They have found no evidence in the past that service providers have any opportunity to learn from feedback about why some sufferers flourish and others fall at the first hurdle. They believe this is why practitioners may take the line that prognosis for a serious mental illness has to be poor. Members suspect this is one of the reasons why undesirable practice tends to go unrecognized. As one carer, who is involved both locally and nationally in the mental health scene, put it:

'Julie's experience [in Chapter 2] only loses its sensationalism and tragedy because we hear of other similar disasters. This is so sad – serious mental illness may be difficult to deal with but a skilled approach reaps rewards for all concerned. There is just no room for complacency and incompetence.' 'So what will it take to change things, then?' someone asked.

A potential specialism?

'Well, I wish we could have an elite of workers – from all disciplines – who could choose to specialize in working with serious mental illness, who could assess individual patients and be available to advise their colleagues as to the most appropriate approach in each case', insisted one carer who has been sure for some time that this is the way forward. A survivor with experience of working in hospitals felt that would be a really good idea. 'Not only could such a scheme benefit sufferers but it would also be a real boost for those who enjoy working with serious mental illness. It's been the unfashionable side of psychiatry for far too long!' 'Yes, and let's remind everyone that any such specialist training should start with input and ideas from those who have been there – that is, those sufferers who have learned all they could about their illness and how to cope with it and who have survived!' exclaimed a carer.

Members of the group had no doubt that they would like to persuade 'those in high places' to pursue the idea of specialist training in working with serious mental illness for those professionals who have shown a real interest in this. They would most certainly want training to include input from sufferers who have found ways of coping with and surviving acute psychosis and also from the families who have supported them in this.

SUMMING UP

Members of the LEAP group found the contrast between Sue's two experiences of hospital to be stark and unacceptable. The group felt that there appears to be considerable evidence to suggest that sufferers may be subjected to one of two types of experience depending on the prevalent culture on the ward and whether or not the team use a judgemental approach to serious mental illness. They found this very worrying as the latter phenomenon seemed to reflect a gradual erosion of understanding and knowledge about the nature of psychosis and the potential of the trauma caused by each episode. Members finished their discussion with a strong recommendation for specialist training across the disciplines for those individuals who have shown a particular interest in developing a sound knowledge base and skills in working with serious mental illness.

INFORMATION

The following pieces of information are relevant to points brought up during the group's analysis and discussion which are highlighted in the text:

(1) A risk of over-dependency

During the worst times of a schizophrenic illness, there is a tendency for sufferers to become very dependent on one other person. This is more often than not the mother or another close relative but sometimes it maybe a formal carer such as a nurse or social worker. This can become an intense and 'clinging' and exclusive relationship, shutting out even other family members living in the same household. In effect, the relationship becomes a 'lifeline' for a sufferer shunning everyone and everything else until better health returns. It is this which makes it helpful for several members of staff, rather than one, to be involved with the patient from the start of a stay in hospital, to avoid any such dependency developing and to open up opportunities for gradually making other social contacts.

(2) A lack of stimulation

As we noted in Chapter 1, the Sainsbury Centre for Mental Health quality of care in acute psychiatric wards survey, carried out between September 1996 and April 1997, involving 215 patients in acute wards throughout England and Wales, revealed that patients complain they are bored during their stay on the ward and few in any are involved in planned programmes of social activity. 40 per cent of all patients involved in this survey undertook no social or recreational activity during their stay in hospital.

A free briefing paper, or a copy of the full report at £9 plus 10 per cent p&p, can be obtained from The Sainsbury Centre for Mental Health, 134–138 Borough High Street, London SE1 1LB.

EXERCISE

Do you believe that the second ward team might have learned more about working with an uncontrolled psychosis if they had

(a) **heeded what family and friends were trying to tell them about the patient?**

(b) **talked through the experience with the patient when she was no longer deluded?**

CHAPTER 6

Getting it right
A lottery?

Two of the three case studies featured in this chapter are concerned with the 'flip-side' of the experiences of sufferers we have met earlier in this book. In Chapter 2, we learned about Julie's experiences during the two years when she first came to the notice of the mental health services. Well on the road to recovery now, we now learn what happened when she was at last allowed to take up the offer of a bed in a specialist NHS unit under the supervision and care of the 'second opinion' psychiatrist. In Chapter 3, we learned about Naomi's experience in an NHS hospital and the unhappy memories this still evokes. We learn here what happened when she moved to a private hospital. Both Julie and Naomi have chosen to tell us about what happened next in their own words.

Barry is the third sufferer we are concerned with in this chapter. here. His full case study was featured in the first book in this series – *Getting Into the System* – and the relevant part of this is repeated here because this young man had dramatically different experiences – like Julie and Naomi – but this time in two wards during one stay in one hospital.

CASE STUDY – PART 2 JULIE REVISITED

A positive experience as an inpatient

'When I went to the second hospital, I was told what my illness was and I was given carefully titrated medication. I knew then that I could get better. I was given hope and encouragement. Both my family and I now had confidence in a competent, compassionate psychiatrist. We felt that he was truthful. He did not make me feel 'bad' or that I was behaving inappropriately – this had so often been the description of my earlier behaviour which was, of course, driven by an untreated psychosis.

'The hospital that I moved to was a long way from my home but the care was very good. It was part of a general hospital. This in itself helped, as there was no connotation of an asylum. In addition, the staff were understanding and had time for me. I was allowed to bring my guitar and shown a bright, cheerful room where I could play it at my leisure. On one or two occasions, my keyworker, who also enjoys playing guitar, joined in. There was an emphasis on self and I was encouraged to do what I wanted and what I felt beneficial in the therapy department.

'I was also encouraged to join a group whose members were all taking the same drug as me and was run by someone also on this medication. I found this very helpful. It was good to know I was not alone. The ward was open-plan and yet there was privacy. All the staff had a good sense of humour. They made it clear they were there for the patients and did not hide away to watch television, smoke and read magazines. The latter, unfortunately, is what I experienced in my previous hospital when I first became ill. There was no bullying and no intimidation. Aggressive physical and verbal exchanges were minimal and I found the atmosphere positive. We had free access to our bedrooms and to the kitchen. Also I got the impression that the staff were partners in our care. Previously I had had experience of bad practice – almost verging on abuse – where professionals were in denial about my illness. The result of this, of course, was disastrous. Instead, in this (second) hospital patients were looked upon as adjunctive to treatment – an essential element in the care package on the ward. My family were always greeted kindly and acknowledged.

'There was no stealing of others' property and any worry or concern was looked into and, if necessary, action was taken. I feel that all this support helped build up my self-esteem. I began to feel that I could get better. We were treated with respect, our illnesses were acknowledged and treated. Previously I had felt judged, denied access to a sick role, and worthless as a result.

'In this hospital, I felt that I was receiving support and active help. I felt that I could get better. As a result, the suicidal feelings I had had evaporated. My family said that they had got their daughter and sister back. I feel so grateful I have now had this experience of good practice with a good team and a caring, knowledgeable consultant. *I truly believe that the main factor in schizophrenia is diagnosis and early treatment* (1).

CASE STUDY – PART 3 NAOMI REVISITED

A positive move

'Ron and his family tried to find out if there was a better place for me to be and, as a result of this, a week after my first admission, I transferred to a private hospital. When we arrived there, Ron was looking terrible. He still had his arm in a sling, had not been able to wash his hair properly because of the stitches in his head, and was still confused about what had been happening to me. One of the nursing staff saw him waiting on his own while I was first being seen by a doctor. She offered him a cup of tea and just placed her hand on his shoulder, the uninjured one that is, to show she knew he was finding everything very tough. He broke down in tears. No-one at the other hospital had indicated in any way that they appreciated he might be having a really bad time.

'The private hospital was different in other ways too. The surroundings were pleasant and the food was good. There was none of the confusion we had felt previously as to who were staff and who were patients. Nurses were in uniform and very approachable and they would also come up and chat with you and answer questions.

My medication was closely monitored and changed if it wasn't working within a reasonable time. I felt looked after. Ron also felt I was being looked after, which I now know was a great comfort to him. His questions were answered. He was able to talk to my psychiatrist and other staff; with me, or on his own.

'It was very nice to have luxuries such as my own shower and television and telephone to make personal calls but, most of all, I enjoyed the space and privacy I was given and the fact that I was treated with dignity and given back some self respect in the midst of all my bizarre behaviour.

'After a few days, during which I was able to rest, a full programme of therapy was arranged to suit my particular needs and I was gently but actively encouraged to participate in this programme. This was reviewed and changed as my mood varied from being manic to being depressed. My recovery was not immediate. I was seriously ill for eighteen months with three manic episodes, each one requiring hospitalization. When not an in-patient, I attended a day centre at the hospital twice a week and had regular sessions with the senior nurse. My appointments with my psychiatrist continued on a monthly basis with one hour sessions. It has been pointed out to me several times that all this must have cost a lot of money. Well, yes, it did! However, my private health care was funded by a generous employer who paid me full pay for six months, half pay for six months and pension rate for the rest. Nevertheless, Ron and I have discussed in depth the expenses involved and we have both agreed that if I ever needed to be in hospital again the number one priority would be to "go private" if at all possible and that includes the use of bank loans, re-mortgaging our house or whatever it takes to achieve it.

'The conditions and environment within the private hospital were, of course, different to that in the NHS hospital. The nice surroundings were a bonus. However, the biggest difference – and to me the most important difference – was the staff; the nurses, the occupational therapy workers and the psychiatrists. They were not necessarily any better at their jobs than their NHS colleagues but the important thing, and the most helpful thing for me, was that they had vastly more time for me. All the staff monitored me more closely, they monitored my medication closely and communicated their observations to each other often and systematically. As a result, I believe that I recovered much more quickly than I would have done had I been left at the first hospital where there was little evidence of close monitoring and apparently little opportunity for staff to get to know me or the way my illness affected me. In fact, I have never really believed I would have survived if I had stayed at the NHS hospital. Of course, both of these last statements are subjective – I can't prove them but it is how it seemed to me at the time and nothing has happened to change my mind since.'

CASE STUDY BARRY REVISITED
(see chapter 4 of *Getting into the System*)
Losing the plot?

This young man was allowed to 'slip through the net' at 17 years of age within months of his psychosis having been recognized by a psychiatrist and two other mental health professionals. Having struggled on without effective help for their son for almost two years,

Barry's parents' pleas for help finally paid off when he was referred to a day centre. The staff at this centre soon expressed their concern about their new client and asked the manager to have a talk with him. A few days later, this was achieved and Barry came limping into the older man's office and although he muttered something about blisters, the manager arranged for a visiting CPN to have a look at these. She in turn was horrified at the state of his feet which were covered with sores and looked as if they had never seen soap and water. She arranged for these to be seen and dressed at the local Accident and Emergency department.

Later, the nurse made a home visit to meet Barry's parents and she found them touchingly grateful to make contact with a health professional once more and they explained that their home had become a war zone. They had learned to keep out of Barry's way as much as possible because he became hostile and aggressive if they approached him. He kept his room locked and his mother left him to help himself to food from the fridge as he would not sit down and eat a meal with them. Similarly, they had had no success in trying to influence his personal hygiene and they were most concerned about this as Barry had been clean, even fastidious, before things had started to go wrong several years ago.

At this point, Barry was referred to the psychiatrist who serviced the centre and the manager invited the parents to come along for the appointment. The specialist told them that Barry had schizophrenia and that he could only be helped in hospital; she would arrange for him to come in as soon as she could make a bed available for him. A month later, Barry was admitted to hospital under Section 3, allowing for up to six months of treatment in hospital.

On admission, the young man was prescribed an anti-psychotic drug. This had happened at the start of his illness too but, confused and delusional, and left to his own devices, he had only taken it for a brief period. This time, he had no choice but to take the medication. He quickly started to make real progress and his parents were delighted to see this. For the first time in a long while, he was prepared to talk with them and they began to see again the son they thought they had lost for ever.

After six weeks or so, Barry's new psychiatrist reported to the parents that she was so pleased with his progress in such a short time that she felt sure he could benefit from a longer stay in hospital so that he could be helped with his damaged social and living skills. She went ahead and arranged for her patient to be transferred to a rehabilitation ward, under the care of one of her colleagues. As it turned out, the parents were not given an opportunity to meet this new psychiatrist but they were not worried about this as they felt sure that after all the misery and delays, Barry had come through the worst of this illness and was now 'on the mend'.

Unfortunately, their new found confidence was misplaced. Within a week of moving onto the new ward, Barry's medication was reduced. When his parents queried this, the nurse in charge told them that their son did not have any illness that required drugs. Horrified, his mother protested that he was now being treated for schizophrenia and they were delighted with the progress he was making. The nurse shrugged her shoulders, saying it seemed more likely that his problems were due to poor family relationships. Stunned, the parents waited for her to enlarge on this statement but this did not happen. Neither was any attempt made by the psychiatrist or his team to meet with the parents to discuss this viewpoint, nor to provide any family sessions.

Once more, Barry started to shun his parents and very soon they were told by ward staff that it was not a good idea for them to visit their son as this only upset him. Three months later, he was discharged to a hostel where he just about coped, avoiding his peers and the staff and regularly going missing at night-time. Eventually, after continued reports from the staff team about the young man's abnormal behaviour, a psychiatrist in the community agreed to raise the dose of his medication to the level being prescribed before his move to the rehabilitation ward. Because of the marked improvement reported by the staff team, the medication was later raised once more. Shortly after this, it was noticeable that Barry started to look forward to his parents' tentative visits and one evening a member of staff telephoned to ask if Barry might pop round and see them? This was the start of regular home visits by a young man now freed from torment and able to enjoy some quality of life for the first time for several years.

COMMENT

Among the cases analysed in this book we have noted a frequently recurring theme of dramatic changes in the fortunes of sufferers which have correlated with a change of hospital, psychiatrist and, or, ward team.

You might feel it worthwhile at this point to pause and consider what might have influenced the markedly different approaches to which Julie, Naomi and Barry were subjected to. Do you find such variations of approach to a serious mental illness to be acceptable?

GROUP'S ANALYSIS OF THESE CASE STUDIES

Members were startled by the contrasts in the experiences of each of these three individuals and their families' impotence to do anything about it when the system so clearly failed them. They decided to look at each of the cases in turn.

Julie

It seemed to the group that many months of this young woman's life had been wasted before she was eventually admitted to the 'second opinion' psychiatrist's specialist ward. First and foremost, they noted her comments about this new doctor; his competence and compassion, his honesty and his emphasis on her illness rather than on the behaviour caused by it. 'Surely, we could reasonably expect these admittedly admirable qualities in any doctor supervising someone with a serious mental illness?' sighed a carer. 'Yes, I quite agree,' nodded a survivor, 'but in her enthusiasm for the second psychiatrist's approach, Julie has rightly highlighted the fact that this isn't the case, hasn't she?'

'Yes, it's the same with the rest of the staff, isn't it?' another member pointed out, 'She mentions about her keyworker and the two of them playing their guitars together. She says confidently that the staff were there for the patients and did not hide away to watch television, smoke and read magazines and all of this says as much about her experience of the staff in the other hospital as it does about this very different, caring team, doesn't it?' 'Yes, and she talks about being respected and encouraged to do what she wanted to do – understandably all of this built up her self-esteem', a survivor commented. A carer summed it up with 'And added to this, her being allowed to do things she's interested in and having the opportunity to join a group of other patients taking the same medication – it really is a recipe for success, isn't it?'

There seemed to be no doubt in members' minds that this was certainly the case. However, for one survivor at least, Julie had mentioned something else which was as important as all these other factors put together:

> 'For me,' she insisted, 'the most serious thing that Julie has said about the earlier experience is about being denied a sick role – being denied the right to be ill and feeling worthless as a result. I truly believe that it is this – the professionals being "in denial" as she puts it – that allows them to be judgemental. This verges on abuse in some cases, she's right about that too.'

'Well, yes', a carer agreed, 'If only someone could persuade individual members of these judgemental ward teams to consider how they would feel if they had, for example, a serious physical illness and they were denied a sick role and told there was nothing wrong with them but their attitude or behaviour. I'm sure they would begin to understand that no-one has the right to deprive someone who is ill from the right to a sick role.' Other members also felt that it was this denial of her illness which caused Julie and her family such misery. 'No wonder she emphasizes the need for diagnosis and early treatment', another carer exclaimed.

A final remark on Julie's testimony summed up everyone's feelings very well with 'Let's have some more doctors and units like this one, please!' In fact, the LEAP group would have liked to have departed at this point from their invariable rule of not revealing names and identities of those involved in case studies in order to pay special tribute to this NHS psychiatrist and his colleagues.

Naomi

Members gasped when they first read Naomi's account of how Ron was looking a week or so after her admission to the first hospital and that it had taken all that time for a member of staff to offer him sympathy. 'The hand on the shoulder must have meant so much to him', exclaimed a carer, 'A relaxing of all that pent up frustration and here was someone identifying with this. No wonder he broke down in tears.'

'Once again', another member observed, 'this act of kindness says more about the staff at that first hospital than it does about those at the second one, doesn't it?' Well, yes, the initial tendency was to think, 'Oh, good!' before realization dawned that this traumatized man had received nothing at all from all the other members of the caring professions he had met day after day since his accident and Naomi's first admission. On further discussing this man's desperate plight during that first week, a member commented,

> 'Interestingly, Naomi goes on to mention another problem for Ron – this confusion over not knowing who were nurses and who were patients and she clearly found it helpful herself when the nurses were in uniform.'

'Yes, but she describes them as being approachable and happy to come up and chat with her too', a survivor pointed out. 'It seems to me that this business about the nurses going "incognito" is only so important because from our experience some of them don't make any attempt to introduce themselves or approach new patients and visitors as they come into the ward!' 'Well, yes,' agreed a carer, 'the message seems to be "work it out for yourselves!" In fact, Naomi is talking about a pro-active approach by the staff as well as a means of identification, isn't she?'

Members were not surprised to note that Naomi also talked with gratitude about being treated with dignity and being given back some self-respect even while she was still behaving in a bizarre way and they were interested to note that the space and privacy she was given mattered so much to her too. One carer commented that she knew that this was beginning to happen in her local hospital now – that patients were being allowed to retreat to the comparative peace of their dormitory sometimes during the day instead of being expected to spend their spare time in a room with the television blaring out all the time, adding 'I could have cried sometimes in the past seeing my son cringing in a corner of the only lounge trying to shut out this deafening noise – I certainly couldn't have put up with it for long but he had no choice in the matter.'

'It's clear too that Naomi appreciated having some stimulating activity just like Julie – and being allowed to feel it was her decision to take part – "I was gently but actively encouraged to participate' says it all!" a survivor laughed. 'Yes, it's all about approach, isn't it?' agreed a carer, 'and Naomi's fair enough to say the staff may have been no better at their jobs than the NHS staff but that they had more time for her and that was what mattered!' 'Hmm, but surely having time for the patients – and in particular having time to get to know them and find out how their illness is affecting them – should be the key part of the staff team's role anyway, shouldn't it?' queried another carer. 'Well you'd think so, wouldn't you?' agreed a survivor, 'and it is probably the only way to learn about what really matters when working with serious mental illness too!'

Although members of the LEAP group had reservations about the fact that Naomi had to go to a private hospital to have such a positive experience, they were very impressed with the service she received. Perhaps a carer summed up their feelings about this with the comment, 'Most people given the choice would no doubt opt for private treatment and maybe that's why we have to monitor the NHS system carefully.' 'Yes, this is important, isn't it?' someone agreed. 'As we noted earlier when we were talking about a "duty to care", families rarely want to make ripples when they're worried about a loved one's treatment but it's probably important that they do, if only to make sure that standards don't drop too far.'

Barry

When members had looked at this young man's case when they were working on *Getting into the System*, they had been horrified at the lack of continuity in treatment and approach when he was transferred to a second ward in the same hospital. They could find no explanation for this and even wondered initially if the second psychiatrist really knew nothing about his new patient. However, they quickly dismissed this possibility when they realized that this doctor would have insisted on a proper referral from his medical colleague on the first ward and that the patient's file would have gone with him when he moved anyway.

This case is different to those in the present book where three sufferers have been subjected to dramatically different treatment and approaches for their illness, ie, Julie, Naomi and Sue. For them this has taken place in different hospitals or at different times. Barry, as we have seen, merely changed wards during one stay in hospital. His medical file should have confirmed the accuracy of the first doctor's diagnosis because he had made such a dramatic improvement in a matter of weeks after 'slipping through the net' two years earlier. Similarly, if the second psychiatrist had had any doubts about his new patient's diagnosis and progress, then he must have had ready access to doctors and the staff team working on the first ward.

'So, what we come down to, is a different culture on this second ward, isn't it? On the first ward, the psychiatrist demonstrates that her initial diagnosis of schizophrenia is correct by successfully treating it with anti-psychotic medication. On the second ward, the psychiatrist and his colleagues say "What's schizophrenia?" Well, that's the way it looks to me, anyway!' this carer insisted.

'And me too', agreed a survivor, 'and it starts with noting Barry's wariness about his parents and questioning him about them and later confirming that they are the problem when he becomes increasingly paranoid and it goes on from there!' 'We're back to scapegoating families for their relative's illness, aren't we?' (2) 'And we could be forgiven for assuming that some psychiatrists and their ward teams have no more regard for their professional colleagues' experience or opinions about a patient then they have for the family's experience or opinions!

It's very sad, isn't it?' concluded a carer. This was the overwhelming feeling about Barry's experience; how sad that just as he was beginning to break through his longstanding psychotic illness and to reach out to his family and those around him again, this could all be snatched away from him again by altering the treatment he had waited for so long.

Earlier, when working on *Getting into the System*, members of the LEAP group were at a loss to understand why the rehabilitation ward team didn't re-think their hasty decision when Barry's condition deteriorated to the point that he had reached before coming into hospital. They found it worrying that the new doctor and his colleagues could have been satisfied with this outcome when the young man had started to make such good progress.

Someone suggested that there was a telling difference in the attitude of the two psychiatrists in this case, pointing out that 'the first doctor was happy for Barry's parents to be present when she assessed their son and she did not hesitate to share with them the diagnosis as she saw it. In contrast, the second doctor didn't bother to introduce himself to the parents or to meet with them later although he and his staff obviously made some sort of critical judgement about their relationship with Barry.' 'Yes, I agree', a survivor joined in. 'This second team were judgmental, weren't they? And they were dismissive about Barry's having a serious mental illness despite the splendid evidence of his rapid progress on anti-psychotic medication. Can it be coincidence that we have seen these judgemental attitudes – with Julie and Sue, as well as with Barry – when the ward team have avoided a medical approach to their patients' problems?'

No, other members did not think this was coincidence and one observed that 'I couldn't agree more. It seems to me that where professionals do not focus in on and recognize the patient's psychotic illness, they come up with all sorts of red herrings about their reason for being in hospital.' 'Well, yes! With Julie, the patient was misbehaving because she was pretending to be schizophrenic. With Sue, she was "acting out" for some reason – any reason other than her schizophrenia being out of control. With Barry, the problem was seemingly the family and they were no sooner given that impression than the judgment became self-fulfilling because without sufficient medication he became paranoid about them again!' concluded a survivor.

Members agreed to return to this vexing subject later and at this point they moved on to their further discussion on several similarities in these cases.

THE WIDER PERSPECTIVE

Members felt that although their experiences were different, Naomi's story resembled Julie's in a lot of ways. 'Surely we're talking here – in both cases – about staff attitudes towards their patients as much as anything else, aren't we?' suggested a carer.

Being respected and listened to

Yes, indeed. It seemed quite clear to members of the group that Naomi and Julie both gave emphasis to having been given dignity and respect during their second stay in hospital. According to Naomi this had been the case even when she was still behaving in a bizarre manner and the LEAP group thought this was a very important achievement and one which could surely be repeated in NHS hospitals? Similarly, Julie talked of the staff being there for the patients and of being given the dignity of a sick role. Members felt that this was something which could certainly be achieved in all NHS hospitals, 'but only when all ward teams accept and recognize serious mental illness', a carer pointed out wryly.

One of the group's younger survivors was impressed with the way both Naomi and Julie mentioned that staff made themselves available and listened to their patients – just like Sue in her first admission to hospital too, she said wistfully. 'Wouldn't it be nice? It sounds like another world to me! I was really pleased when a nurse said to me the last time I went into hospital that if ever I wanted to talk to someone she would listen. However, before I could reply, she added that I must understand that I would have to approach her first because she would not come to me; no matter how distressed I was. So that was that – it's bad enough talking about my awful experiences when I'm like that anyway – you need encouragement when you're psychotic, not a challenge!'

'Where on earth was that nurse coming from?' queried another survivor. 'Oh, dear', she added, 'I do so wish that just once some of these professionals with these odd ideas could have a flash of appreciation of what it means to be psychotic – what it means to the poor soul trying to cope with it!'

Families being respected and listened to

Members felt that in Barry's case, the family were treated appallingly by the second psychiatrist and ward team and recalled that Joe's (see Chapter 4) had fared no better. By contrast, both Julie and Naomi paid testimony to the way their loved ones were treated during their second experience of hospital, as did Sue when she spoke of her first stay in hospital. 'There's no rhyme or reason to it all, is there?' asked a carer, 'it's quite clear that it's nothing more than a lottery how families are treated, let alone the patients!' 'Well, I'm not sure I agree with that – I believe a pattern is emerging', a survivor observed, 'in the cases we've been looking at, anyway. With the exception of Joe – and we've not really been able to work out what goes on in his case, have we? – all the others seem to correlate. What I mean by that is, if the patient's experience is a positive one, then their families are treated properly too.'

Rather intrigued, members paused to take a further look at this and indeed found that when Naomi felt she was neglected, her husband was ignored too. Similarly, when Julie was ill and unhappy, the ward team took no notice of what her relatives had to say or wanted for her. On the ward where Barry was allowed to deteriorate, his parents were given to understand that he suffered from the effects of family relationships rather than an illness and they were later asked not to visit the ward. When Sue was neglected, her family's and friends' testimonies were ignored, as was her husband even when she was well again. When each of these patients had a good experience and were flourishing, their families were also treated with respect and listened to. 'Well', laughed a carer, 'let that be a lesson to everyone! Seriously, though,' she added, 'I'm sure we're back to everything falling into place when teams are non-judgemental and focus on the patient's illness and everything going horribly wrong when they are judgemental and looking for explanations other than illness.'

The LEAP group felt that these conclusions were very important and would bear detailed investigation by any service providers interested in trying to standardize quality of care. Members went on at this point to look once more at the possible origins of ward teams' attitudes towards serious mental illness.

A question of attitudes?

'But are we talking about attitudes or about ignorance on the subject of serious mental illness?' a carer asked. 'In Julie's case, the staff in the first hospital seem to think that a hitherto normal and successful young woman had nothing better to do than to pretend to be psychotic and, in Naomi's case, the staff in the first hospital seem to think it was someone else's role to communicate with their patients, let alone offer them care and protection.' 'Yes, and that second example is not just about training, is it?' agreed a second carer. 'After all, nurses all have the same training, don't they? So we could expect them to have the similar attitudes too but the staff in the specialist unit and in the private hospital seem very different, don't they?'

A question of expectations?

'I've been thinking about this', another carer commented, 'and it seems to me that it must have something to do with employers' expectations of their staff. I believe that those responsible for a specialist unit or running a private hospital have no choice but to ensure that certain standards are adhered to – I mean this is a must if you're running a business or building up a reputation for possessing exceptional skills and knowledge!' 'Well, yes that's right, isn't it?' agreed a survivor, 'and if your patients are spending a small fortune on their treatment and care, they're not going to be too impressed with being kept in hospital indefinitely because the doctors have decided they're feigning a psychotic illness or "acting out" or whatever!'

This, at last, brought some welcome light relief as well as bringing everyone back to basics and a realization that specialist units and private hospitals need to look for obvious explanations of bizarre behaviour and avoid unnecessary delays in treating their patients. Yes, it seemed that employers' expectations could very much influence the way that the various disciplines might wish to approach a serious mental illness. 'Apart from anything else, it would seem reasonable to suppose that professionals working in a specialist unit or a private hospital might be much more interested in sharing one approach and pooling knowledge and skills than in preserving the differences between them and this must be important too', concluded a carer thoughtfully. Yes, members were very much inclined to believe that a practical, down-to-earth approach would be a must in the private sector and in a specialist unit. 'When all is said and done', a survivor pointed out, 'people expect results in these situations, don't they?'

A readily available resource?

Members were cheered when someone reminded everybody that Sue's first experience in hospital had been very similar in quality and care to Julie's and Naomi's second experiences and they agreed when he claimed 'so it can happen in a setting without any sort of special status or funding. It may be that Sue's experience is more typical of the early and mid 1980s than anything we might see now but its major ingredient – that is, "loving care" – can't really have become just another scarce resource, surely?'

Well, no, the LEAP group hoped not! In an earlier chapter, they had paused for a moment to sing the praises of professionals whose dedication and loving care is beyond question. At this point, it seemed not only apt but important to turn away from all the variables currently found in the handling of a serious mental illness and to focus instead on the one 'major ingredient' of a stay in hospital – that is, the quality of care – which they consider should be standard throughout the system. See Chapter 7 for further discussion of this subject.

SUMMING UP

Members of the group were happy to learn that Julie and Naomi eventually had good experiences with, in each case, a change of psychiatrist, ward team and hospital. Nevertheless, they wished these good experiences could have been achieved in an ordinary NHS setting, particularly as both patients cited issues such as (a) being treated with respect and (b) staff making themselves available to patients as the important ones.

They were sad to note again that, after years of neglected illness, Barry's rapid progress had been sabotaged by a second doctor and ward team who were content to eventually discharge him from hospital no more well than when he was admitted. In particular, this case convinced the LEAP group that 'getting it right' is certainly a lottery as things stand at present.

After some thought about this, members came to the conclusion that those ward teams who had a positive attitude towards families were the same ones who provided a good quality of treatment and care for patients. The LEAP group would like to think that someone responsible for service provision might be interested enough to investigate this potentially rewarding hypothesis!

Finally, when one member of the group suggested that 'loving care' was the major ingredient to be found in Julie's, Naomi's and Sue's more positive experiences in hospital, it was decided that a whole chapter should be dedicated to 'quality of care' (see Chapter 7).

INFORMATION

The following pieces of information are relevant to points brought up during the group's analysis and discussion which have been highlighted in the text:

(1) Early diagnosis and treatment

(a) A large extended study of first episodes of schizophrenia revealed that the most important determinant of relapse was the duration of illness prior to starting neuroleptic medication (Crow, T.J. *et al.* (1986) 'The Northwick Park study of first episodes of schizophrenia, part II: A randomized controlled trial of prophylactic neuroleptic treatment.' *British Journal of Psychiatry 148*, 120–127).

(b) Not long after Crow (1986) was published, workers conducting a follow-up study of schizophrenia across North America, claimed that it may take only one year of active illness for deterioration or a 'threshold of chronicity' to be reached (McGlashan, T.H. (1988) 'A Selective review of recent North American long-term follow-up studies of schizophrenia.' *Schizophrenia Bulletin 14*, 4, 515–542).

(c) A Tokyo University study showed that patients who had had symptoms longer than 1 year before entering treatment were more likely to relapse than patients who were treated within the year (Anzai, N. *et al.* (1988) 'Early neuroleptic medication within one year after onset can reduce risk of later relapses in schizophrenic patients.' *Annual Report Pharmacopysychiatric Research Foundation 19*, 258–265).

(d) Richard Jed Wyatt has concluded, in his comprehensive overview of the use of neuroleptic medication and the natural course of schizophrenia, that 'some patients are left with a damaging residual effect if a psychosis is allowed to proceed unmitigated. While psychosis is undoubtedly demoralising and stigmatising, it may also be biologically toxic' (Wyatt, R.J. (1991) 'Neuroleptics and the natural course of schizophrenia.' *Schizophrenia Bulletin 17*, 2).

(e) A study of 70 schizophrenia patients revealed that poorer outcome was associated with longer duration of untreated psychosis. Duration of psychotic symptoms was the only variable significantly associated with poorer outcome (Lieberman, J.A. *et al.* (1992) 'Prospective study of psychobiology in first-episode schizophrenia at Hillside Hospital.' *Schizophrenia Bulletin 18*, 3).

(f) Finally, Max Birchwood, clinical psychologist, and colleagues claim that what is needed is a complementary approach, which focuses on the early phase of psychosis, with intervention strategies dedicated to 'what we have argued could be a critical period both biologically and psychosocially' (Birchwood, M., McGorry, P. and Jackson, H. (1997) 'Early intervention in schizophrenia.' *British Journal of Psychiatry 170*, 2–5).

(2) The 'family theories'

During the 1960s and 1970s there was an abundance of theories of a similar kind which blamed the families of schizophrenia sufferers for their relative's illness. These dominated much of the literature and received wisdom of the time and added significantly to the misery of families trying to cope with living with a serious mental illness. They were officially discredited and abandoned because, among other things, researchers were discovering for the first time the idiosyncrasies of normal family life rather than anything unusual about families coping with schizophrenia. The theories have nevertheless influenced for many years the attitudes of some of those who in turn have influence over the training and supervision of recruits to the caring professions; those interested in this phenomenon may like to read Christine Heron's chapter on mental health carers in *Working with Carers*, 1998. London: Jessica Kingsley Publishers.

For a full discussion and useful references on the family theories, see Gwen Howe (1991) *The Reality of Schizophrenia*. London: Faber & Faber, pp.79–81.

EXERCISE

There seems to be little doubt that the rejection of the 'medical model' in psychiatry has led to the adoption by some professions of theories and approaches to psychosis which do not emphasize illness.

Do you believe this to be in the best interests of sufferers and those closest to them who still have to persevere with finding ways of coping with a serious mental illness regardless of the varying opinions of the different professionals they meet up with along the way?

CHAPTER 7

An acceptable quality of care?

A recurring theme in this book has highlighted the sort of difference in treatment and care that any one sufferer may experience during different episodes of the same serious mental illness. In earlier chapters, the LEAP group has considered possible reasons for this startling variation in approach to this type of illness. In this chapter, however, members have decided to focus on what they believe should be a baseline for acceptable standards of care for psychiatric patients while in hospital regardless of the approach taken to their illness. To this end, we have grouped together, under various headings, comments and observations offered by members of the LEAP group and their families while they have been working on earlier chapters in this book. In doing this, material has been selected which has so far not been used in this text and it is hoped that this chapter will provide a more realistic 'feel' of what it is like to be an inpatient on a modern acute psychiatric ward than we could have provided by considering another individual case study.

About respect

Members of the LEAP group always list respect as their first priority, ie that sufferers and their families should be shown respect. It may be that most readers would take it for granted that seriously ill patients are treated with respect and, indeed, this was the case with one young relative of a sufferer who commented:

'I've grown up in a society which projects negative attitudes towards the old mental hospitals – basically, all about decaying buildings filled with decaying people! Certainly, my first visit to such a hospital seemed to confirm this. However, since then I've been shocked to find that the things which seem to upset patients who have been unhappy in hospital have not been about their surroundings but about the way they've been treated on the ward.'

Another member gave us a very worrying example of this phenomenon:

'I'll never forget the morning my son was discharged from a ward where he had been treated well on previous admissions. When my husband and I arrived, the psychiatrist greeted us with "Oh, good, you've come to fetch your little psychopath!" This was in front of him. That was the only time my son has ever been treated in that way – I noted that things went back to how they used to be when there was a change of ward manager.'

Two other carers in the group each cited other examples of a disrespectful, uncaring attitude by ward staff which have upset them. One told us, 'Ward "X" is for particularly ill patients and when my relative was there respect didn't come into it – the biscuits which accompanied the bedtime drinks were scoffed by the nurses before the patients could get to them and the latter were also told that the television was for the staff and not for them – it was all a big wind-up really.' The other told us 'A nurse came into the lounge on "Y" ward with a big grin and announced "bed!", turning off the TV in the middle of the last episode in a series which everyone knew the patients had been watching and talking about for the past two months. Can you imagine the way they felt about this and the frustration it caused?'

Still on the subject of the patient's right to respect, one carer's comment was particularly interesting:

'If I could demand one change it would be for patients' dignity to be respected. There are far too many comments made in front of them which I consider to be degrading, usually by staff but occasionally by relatives too!'

Food for thought for everyone there?

When families talk about a patient's dignity – and this tends to be a recurring topic – they are very often referring to their distress at seeing a particularly ill relative whose appearance and personal hygiene has been neglected in hospital. A carer whose relative has been in hospital for many years put it this way:

'It depends on the nurse, of course – some are very good – but on the whole, there is not nearly enough attention given to appearance and personal hygiene when patients are too ill to take care of themselves. I can't understand why this is not a recognized part of nursing care.'

Another carer whose relative has been in hospital many times over the years said:

'Some nurses do something about it when patients are too ill to wash and look after themselves, but usually far too late in my opinion.'

One mother, whose son is encouraged to come home most weekends, felt driven to tell a charge nurse recently, 'if no-one has persuaded or helped my son to bath and wash his hair by the time I ring next Friday, then he will have to stay on the ward.' She went on to say, 'I had just returned from my long-awaited trip to Australia and you wouldn't believe the state he was in – it's very upsetting and so unnecessary.'

A member of the LEAP group still feels deep disgust for what happened to her during her first breakdown:

'I was so very ill. I lay in a hospital bed not eating nor drinking for days and only used the toilet when my family came in and they would then wheel me down on a commode and sit me on a toilet and try and clean me up. On one occasion my sister screamed at the nurse in charge that I could do with a bath and I was then bathed by two student nurses. Things improved after that, but what if my family hadn't been around? I leave that to your imagination; it's just too disgusting to contemplate!'

It is not surprising that members of the group were very grieved to hear that their very able and self-sufficient young colleague could have been allowed to sink to these depths in hospital. It was a relief to hear at this point of a happier report. A carer told us:

'When I think back on those dreary, sad years when he was in hospital most of the time, one thing stands out – the day I walked onto the ward to see a male nurse gently cutting my relative's claw-like toe nails. All our efforts to get him to cut them himself or let us do it for him had failed but now it smartened him up and made him feel comfortable. He was pleased and it made us feel he was being *looked after.*'

More about respect

In previous chapters, we noted that Julie, Naomi and Sue all stressed the importance of feeling they were respected by the teams supervising their care; this came up as a priority each time. It is interesting to note, therefore, that they also showed concern about the way that their families and friends were treated too. A member of the LEAP group who is a survivor told us of her concern that:

> 'When I visit "Z" Ward, not only do I find fellow sufferers are being treated as second class citizens – being treated as "nutty" by some of the nurses, I've now learned that one well sufferer has had to complain officially about staff treating him disrespectfully when he visited a friend on this ward.'

A carer told us how she felt when she needed to seek reassurance for her son who was very vulnerable at the time and an inpatient:

> 'My only contact with staff during the three months he was in there was when I had to knock on the door of the office where they all congregated. My son was very agitated about something and I needed to allay his fears. I felt I was intruding on their domain and I felt quite intimidated. Someone should have been available to talk to the carers and patients during visiting time.'

Finally, and rather differently, a working mother who is a member of the LEAP group and whose son has now been in hospital for over ten years, made a point that has been brought up by other carers several times in the group's discussions:

> 'I would like to think that the psychiatrist and rest of the ward team would have some respect for my need to have a life of my own as well as being at home for my son. Just occasionally I have the chance to go to a wedding or just go shopping with an old friend and, like most people, I also have times when I am not well or badly needing a rest. Most times I am happy for my son to come home but I am not given the chance to say "No, next weekend won't be convenient" before my son is on the phone telling me it's been agreed he's coming home and I am to fetch him at whatever time. A quick telephone call just to check beforehand that it would be convenient for me would be courteous and very much appreciated but it's never ever happened.'

Being listened to

A natural part of being treated with respect is to be listened to. Psychiatric patients often find that no-one listens to them even when decisions are being made which are of paramount importance to them. A member of the LEAP group winced as she told us of the only real problem she has had with her longstanding schizophrenic illness:

'Not long ago my psychiatrist retired and the new one changed my diagnosis in the middle of my breakdown, prescribing different medication to the one I had always had before. I was very concerned but found I could not compete with medical opinion, although it turned out to be misjudged. It took more than a year of misery for me before this doctor's mistake was put right. He took no notice of my previous psychiatrist's record of successfully treating my breakdowns and he wasn't interested in my opinion either.'

Similarly, a carer told us what happened to her son when he had just been sectioned by a psychiatrist who was a stranger to him:

'When the doctor said he was going to prescribe a certain drug, my son told him that this drug had once made him very ill and he knew this was reported in his notes. The doctor nevertheless prescribed the drug and the results were so awful that there is now a warning about it on the cover of his file. Why couldn't he listen to my son? Does he believe that having a serious mental illness makes the patient into a simpleton?'

Rather differently, one survivor tells a salutary tale about her struggle to persuade a succession of ward teams that the diagnosis given to her by her psychiatrist was right. Despite her own long reluctance to believe she had a schizophrenic illness, she was way ahead of her doctor's professional colleagues in achieving this:

'Hospital staff always insisted I must spend hours with them delving into my past to find a reason for my latest relapse when the real reason was that I had cut down or stopped my medication. But they didn't want to know about this when I told them. Instead we had to look for an underlying reason! Each time I ended up believing them – as I became well again on the medication – and we found "a trigger" for why I was "behaving this way" as they put it. I would leave hospital knowing I was now cured, so why not stop the medication and get on with my life? And that's what I did at the first opportunity each time. Why couldn't they have listened instead of foisting their ideas on me?'

A survivor gave us a friend's account of how she had walked into a psychiatric maternity unit to find her daughter hysterical:

'She had just about managed to struggle through her pregnancy without medication to save her baby from any possible risk. She had been put back on her injections that morning and ward staff were refusing to provide a bottle for her hungry, screaming baby, saying my daughter was being difficult and refusing to continue to breastfeed. When I pointed out to the nurse in charge that she mustn't breastfeed now she was on medication again, I was told I "really shouldn't fill her up with all these silly ideas" (1). Staff, whose knowledge about such basic matters was so remarkably lacking, showed no interest in anything either of us had to say, let alone any consideration for my daughter's rights as a mother. Fortunately, sanity prevailed when I contacted her psychiatrist.'

The nurse's response to this mother led on to another matter which comes up frequently in the LEAP group's discussions – that is, the continued wasting of a valuable resource, ie, the family and others who are close to sufferers when they are well.

More about being listened to

A survivor told us that she feels so strongly about this matter that:

'If I could make just one change to the Mental Health Act, this would be for hospital staff to have to listen to and record what families have to say about the patient and what they would like to happen. I believe that their experience and opinion should be taken into account.'

Another survivor commented:

'I don't understand why no-one takes any notice of my family when they visit me in hospital and try to speak with the staff. Instead, they are ignored despite the fact that they are the people I choose to spend my life with and they are the ones who know me best!'

A parent in the group despaired of any improvements in this direction and gave one example:

'Despite our asking again and again over the previous two weeks for the ward team to do something about extending our son's 28-day section because he was clearly still very paranoid. Instead, they let it elapse and as soon as he realized this had happened he was away! He arrived home in the early hours of the morning, having walked many, many miles in the dark. He was exhausted, shivering, dishevelled and distressed. When I rang them four hours after he'd left the ward, they hadn't even noticed he was missing. Later, someone had to come out to our home to persuade him to return to the hospital.'

Another carer, a 'nearest relative' who has built up considerable expertise over the years because she has really had no choice in the matter, reported:

'The third time my son was admitted to hospital I was challenged in the middle of a sentence as to what I knew about schizophrenia by the doctor and I have often felt that the staff have treated me with some amusement or contempt as if I knew nothing. When I later expressed my concern that my son was making very threatening remarks about members of staff on the ward, this seemed to be treated with amusement too. As it was, they had to listen in the end when someone else made them see this was a serious matter.'

Another mother felt that if families were listened to this would save a lot of misery and a lot of money for the mental health services:

'When things were at their worst for us, our opinions of our child counted for nothing. We were "getting things out of proportion", "over-reacting" or "dysfunctional as a family", but a long time later, we were proved right; he'd been very ill all along.'

Finally, a mother in the LEAP group told us how hospital staff over the years have kept ignoring comments made in her son's file years before, acknowledging his special need for side-effect medication. Worse, they ignored the patient when he pointed this out and they usually ignored her too. Perhaps we can understand, therefore, why she was overwhelmed recently when one of the present ward team protested on her son's behalf:

'This nurse was very angry when he returned from holiday to find that yet again my son's side effect tablets had been cut. The nurse didn't rest until this had been put right and I realized that someone at last understood the misery my son goes through when they do this and just how much his quality of life can be helped by two of these tablets each day. Why should he have to suffer even more than necessary? I was so grateful to this man!'

About information and explanations

Having considered the right to be listened to for both patients and carers, we now come to the need for two-way communication and the need to be told. Again and again members of the LEAP group mention their concern about sufferers and families having to find ways of coping when they are left in ignorance about the things they need to know. As we have seen, this subject comes up regularly when the patient's diagnosis is the topic of conversation. Interestingly, we noted in Chapter 1 that patients on acute psychiatric wards in a recent piece of research complained they are not given enough information about their illness (2).

We have also noted that a lack communication on the part of professionals is sometimes is excused on a 'confidentiality' basis and a member of the LEAP group who is continuously involved with sufferers and their families reports a recent experience which demonstrates just how far this concept can be stretched:

'A woman approached me recently – her son had just been diagnosed as having schizophrenia and is now being sent home to his mother on regular weekend leave. The ward staff have refused to tell her anything about his medication because her son said he didn't want his mother to know when they asked him. However, it seems he is happy to spend every weekend with her and the ward team certainly want him to do this!'

The rest of the group marvelled that a mother could be expected to care for her son for virtually a third of every week without being given any information about his medication. As one carer put it, 'almost by definition, and at least while still ill enough to be in hospital, patients with schizophrenia are reluctant to take medication – which is probably why he doesn't want his mother to know about it! Do the hospital staff just leave it to a newly diagnosed patient to take or leave his medication on the ward? Of course they don't, but that's what's expected of the mother apparently!' 'Well, yes', the first member came back. 'The local mental health team manager has told the mother that the ward staff were justified in their action – you know, the confidentiality thing – if the patient doesn't want his family to know about his illness or treatment, then that's that. Some professionals I've spoken to about this don't agree and have told me that it's up to the ward team to explain to the son that the mother needs to know and understand about the medication – for his sake as well as hers. In other words it's up to the ward team to mediate in the interests of common sense as well as protecting their patient's future welfare. I shouldn't think there could be much doubt about that!'

It is common for families to have to concern themselves with trying to find out something about the illness and how best to support their relative and avoid further breakdown. As we have seen already in this book, this can be a real problem in itself. In the first book of this series – *Getting into the System* – we reported that some of the members of the LEAP group took part in a survey of a local carers' group in 1994 in which respondents highlighted nine services which they felt should be a priority at the time of a first episode of a serious mental illness. Six of these nine services were concerned with the receiving of information and over 80 per cent of respondents received none of these services when their relative was first ill (3). One of these priorities was concerned with letting sufferers have the information they need as and when they are ready for this, usually as they are beginning to recover from a first episode of their illness. Members insist that this is important but that it should be done sensitively and positively (4).

About a proper welcome on the ward

While on the subject of first episodes of a serious mental illness, we have noted earlier in this book how unsatisfactory an admission to hospital can be, whether it is at the time of a first breakdown or a later relapse. The subject frequently comes up in the LEAP group's discussions and at one of these a survivor told us:

'I have always been made to feel welcome on admission to hospital. I have sometimes got hugs from staff I have met previously on the ward. I guess you can't ask for a better welcome than that? I certainly haven't felt I've been treated disrespectfully in hospital either but I may have been lucky in that!'

No-one could top this and members were delighted to hear this warming testimony. The group feels that the way this welcome is handled is very important. Being admitted to a psychiatric ward with a serious mental illness can be a very traumatic experience for sufferers and those closest to them. Perhaps it is an indication of how often this is forgotten, that a member of the LEAP group who is a carer and a frequent visitor to his local hospital to offer support to new sufferers regarded the following experience as the most impressive example of good practice that he has come across:

> 'Hearing a nurse in an acute ward saying "If there is anything you need to know, or need help with now or later, please ask me or another member of the ward staff" to a newly admitted patient and their family, while showing them where all the ward facilities were. This has always served as a memorable approach which our consumer group now cites when we are asked for examples of good practice.'

This member is describing an approach most of us might feel to be appropriate and normal – it incorporates a courteous welcome to a newcomer, together with explanations about the available facilities. It also makes it clear that the patient and family are invited to ask if they have any queries or problems during the patient's stay. However, several members of the LEAP group have been left to 'get on with finding out what is what' and have found this all the more difficult when there is no indicator as to who are staff members and who are patients. A survivor commented on her first admission to hospital:

> 'There was no welcome onto the ward and this was made more difficult by staff not being in uniform; not even wearing badges as a method of identification. There were no explanations of procedure or the things I needed to know – like what would happen in the morning, etc. My family fared no better.'

Another member observed:

> 'The more I think about it, the more impressed I am now about my son's first admission to hospital six years ago. More time was spent with him than at any other time since. Everything was made quite

clear to him from the start, and to us. Visits home went smoothly and I was made to feel welcome at all times. It's not been like that since.'

Her testimony covers more than just the welcome given her son so it may well be that a proper welcome that aims to make newcomers feel at ease during a very difficult time is all part of a complete package of good practice? Sadly, this seems to have been a 'one off' experience for this family.

An observation from another carer painfully revealed how she feels about each new admission:

'When, exhausted after desperate weeks of trying to get help for him last time, I entered the ward with my relative, my first thought was "Don't the staff have any idea at all of what this is like? Can't they identify with the horror of it, the feeling of guilt, the feeling of letting him down, the feeling of shame that I should be driven to this yet again and my aching, unfulfilled need for someone to say, "Well done, stop worrying, he will be alright now!"'

'I've thought about this since', she went on, 'and realized, no, they can't have any idea. I suspect that not one moment of their professional training touches on the unbelievable trauma carers go through again and again. If it did, we'd all be pulling together to avoid these ghastly crisis situations, wouldn't we? As it is we only ever reach this point by the time my relative is raging mad, through no fault of his own.'

Perhaps the type of welcome patients and their carers receive on the ward is particularly important as it needs to encompass the features we have discussed above; features which include the right to feel respected, the right to be listened to and the right to know about what is going on and what one can expect?

About a duty to care and protect

Finally, and possibly most important of all, we come to the patient's need for care and protection. We noted in Chapter 3 that some ward teams don't seem to acknowledge a duty to care and protect vulnerable patients from themselves during their illness when they are psychotic. Most of us might expect this to be a priority for teams supervising the care of patients while they are out of touch with reality, but this does not always seem to be the case. One member of the LEAP group quoted what a colleague at work has told him about trying to support a friend who sufferers with manic depression:

> 'After several costly breakdowns, she asked me to look after her bank books and cheque books so that she can't spend all her money when she becomes high. Nevertheless the last time she was in hospital, my friend was allowed to run up horrendous bills, sending flowers and hampers to famous people on both sides of the Atlantic – people she only knew by name – and when one of the retailers became worried and contacted the hospital they were told, "That's OK – that's her right."'

This man has come to the conclusion that 'civil liberties issues' (5) are used as an excuse for staff to neglect their duty to protect their patients from their illness. This viewpoint would seem to be quite valid in the circumstances and, as such, must surely be a cause for concern. How and why is it that patients needing care and protection from the excesses of a psychotic illness have seemingly lost the right to this care and protection in the eyes of some mental health service providers?

COMMENT

Perhaps it could be argued that the above discussion is all about claiming that the victims of serious mental illness should be treated as first-class citizens with the same rights as everyone else? This would seem to be reasonable and, indeed, members of the LEAP group would claim that sufferers and carers are often in need of more caring and respect at times of breakdown than the rest of society.

It might be worthwhile pausing for a moment to take a further look at what members of the group have had to say up to now in this chapter. Bearing in mind that not one of these examples refers to the pressurized inner-city hospitals we rightly hear so much about in the late 1990s, perhaps you would like to make a note of any of the group's concerns which you would wish to challenge, giving your reasons for this?

A SUMMARY OF THE EXPERIENCES

A need for the patient to receive respect

We have noted members' comments about their concern that the patient's need for respect seems to be too often overlooked. One relative expressed her amazement when she realized that when patients had a negative experience in hospital it was usually because of the way they had been treated on the ward by the staff rather than anything to do with, for example, dismal, run-down surroundings. This discussion led on to the despair of families whose relatives' personal appearance and hygiene are allowed to deteriorate to the point of loss of dignity. One very well survivor in the group shared with us her own experience of just how dire this sort of neglect could be, see p.104.

A need for the patient's family and visitors to receive respect

The subject of the patient's need for respect led to the LEAP group's concern that respect should be shown to those who visit the patient as well. Three of the subjects of case studies in this book stressed how much this mattered to them. In this chapter, a survivor has pointed out that on one ward where she visits patients are treated as second-class citizens by some nurses and a well sufferer was treated no better when he visited a friend on the ward.

We also noted a working mother's claim that the ward team looking after her son should respect her need to have a life of her own to the extent that she might choose to have a weekend to herself just occasionally – this point about weekend leave for patients being taken for granted regardless of carers' needs to lives of their own, albeit very limited, crops up frequently but, inexplicably, remains unacknowledged by many hospital staff teams.

A need for the patient to be listened to

We heard no less than four examples of patients' views being ignored by professionals with potentially catastrophic results, including one where a mother was admonished for filling her daughter up with silly ideas; this despite the fact that both mother and daughter were stating a well-known and important fact. They were right and the ward team were frighteningly wrong but they dealt with this by saying their patient was being difficult and her mother was influencing her in this.

A need for the patient's loved ones to be listened to

We noted that survivors in the LEAP group cared so deeply about this issue that one would like the Mental Health Act to make it mandatory for ward teams to listen to and to record information offered by those usually closest to the patient. Another survivor could not understand why hospital teams did not want to hear what her family – 'those who know me best' – had to say.

Nevertheless, carers in the group made it clear that they are disillusioned on this issue and that they were not expecting anything to change. Complaints ranged from ward teams treating them as 'over-reacting' or 'getting things out of proportion' through to their ignoring carers' reminders that facts about the patient's reaction to drugs, etc, were being overlooked despite being recorded in the medical file.

A need to know

It is quite clear that if patients and their families are to cope with a serious mental illness then they need to be given sufficient information to make this possible. We had already noted earlier in this book that teams such as the one treating Joe, in Chapter 4, and Naomi, in Chapter 3, appear to make no communication whatsoever with families, and in the latter case at least, with patients either.

We also learned from a member of the LEAP group that essential information about her newly diagnosed son was being withheld from a mother who was expected to have him home on weekend leave each week. For members, this was one of those examples of adhering to the 'concept of confidentiality' to a point where it takes precedence over the needs of the patient and the mother he is happy to visit each week.

A need to receive a proper welcome on the ward

We learned about the very positive experiences of one survivor in the group describing warm welcomes from the same ward team on her various admissions. We also noted that a regular visitor to the wards of his local hospital describing the welcome he heard one nurse giving a new patient and their family as the one of the most positive experiences he has come across in the present system. However, it has to be worrying that this seemed to be an exceptional experience in his eyes and those of several of his fellow LEAP group members. One member said she was not welcomed to the ward when she first became ill, nor was she or her family told anything about the ward or its procedures or what she could expect. A carer spoke enthusiastically about her son's first admission to hospital six years earlier but, sadly, had experienced nothing similar since. Finally, another carer spoke of the devastation she felt each time her relative had to be admitted to hospital and her longing for ward staff to realize what this meant to her and how much she needed support at this point and the reinforcement of being told that she had done the right thing and her relative would be alright now.

A need for care and protection

As we have noted earlier in this book, this is a matter which concerns members of the LEAP group as much as any other. In this chapter, we heard about a hospital team which stands by while a patient spends enormous amounts of money on strangers because it is her 'right', even though she asks a friend to keep hold of her bank and building society books so that she can't spend all of her money when she is out of touch with reality. This friend talks of neglect, not 'rights', and members have no doubt at all that this viewpoint is justified in such circumstances.

SOME RECOMMENDATIONS

Members of the LEAP group have decided to apply themselves to those issues raised in this chapter and – under similar headings – to make recommendations they believe to be important. They hope that these may provoke an open debate on ways of moving towards a more satisfactory standardization of quality of care than is being reported by patients admitted to psychiatric wards during the last decade in this century:

(1) A need for respect

The LEAP group recommends that patients and their visitors should be treated with courtesy and respect at all times, with particular emphasis on maintaining the dignity of patients who are too ill to look after their personal care and hygiene.

(2) A need to be listened to

The LEAP group recommends that ward teams should be required to listen to patients – and to those normally close to them when they are well – when they offer information about the patient's psychiatric history and/or normal lifestyle and that these details should always be acknowledged and recorded.

(3) A need to know

The LEAP group recommends that ward teams should be required to share the sort of information which can empower patients and carers to use their own coping skills and to avoid further breakdown. Rights to confidentiality should be treated sensitively and mediation should be made available where such rights conflict with health and welfare issues of all concerned. In particular, members feel it should be a mandatory requirement for ward teams to provide patients and families with contact numbers for the organizations in the voluntary sector which specialize in providing support and information for those having to cope with a serious mental illness.

The addresses and telephone numbers of the Manic Depression Fellowship and the National Schizophrenia Fellowship are included under 'Useful Addresses' at the back of this book, together with others which may be more relevant for some patients and their families.

(4) A need to receive a proper welcome on admission to the ward

The LEAP group recommends that it should be hospital policy (a) to supply patients, before or on their arrival on the ward, with written information on its procedures and facilities and (b) for a member of staff to extend a welcome and answer any immediate queries the patient or family may have.

(5) A need for care and protection

The LEAP group recommends that all hospital teams should be alerted to a 'duty to care and to protect' their patients from the known risks of their illness, including the excesses of a manic episode. In this respect, they also recommend that staff be reminded that 'civil rights issues' should not be used as an excuse for allowing the harmful features of a psychosis to adversely affect a patient's future welfare.

SUMMING UP

In this chapter, members of the LEAP group have, for the first time in this series, focused on their own experiences rather than on those featured in any one case study. In doing this, they have concentrated on the potential 'caring' component of 'hospital treatment and care' because they are particularly concerned about the differing levels of care which they know about and which have become more evident while working on this series and on this book in particular. The group feel that a variation of approaches towards psychosis should not be allowed to affect the quality of care received by any one patient with a serious mental illness. In fact, as one carer put it, 'we are talking here about "doing unto others as you would have them do unto you"', and it is in this spirit that the consumer has decided to speak on this pressing matter.

INFORMATION

The following pieces of information are relevant to points brought up in this chapter and which have been highlighted in the text.

(1) Breastfeeding and medication

There is little agreement as to whether or not neuroleptic medication taken in a mother's pregnancy can affect the foetus. Perhaps understandably, those who market the drugs have little to say on the subject and in the present climate where most doctors advise pregnant mothers not to take even headache pills if they can avoid this, it is not surprising that women with schizophrenia are encouraged not to take their medication during pregnancy.

The young mother cited in this case achieved this with some real difficulty. She was then accused, at a time when she was very vulnerable because her illness was not yet controlled, of being difficult and unco-operative when she refused to breastfeed her baby once she had been reinstated on the medication. There are, of course, no doubts at all that the risks of passing on the effects of drugs through a mother's milk are well recognized and manufacturers certainly caution against breastfeeding while taking this particular type of medication.

(2) A right to know

Acute Problems – a survey of the quality of care in acute psychiatric wards in England and Wales carried out by the Sainsbury Centre for Mental Health – reveals that nearly half of the 215 inpatients featured in this research complained that they had not received enough information about their illness and the possible treatments. A free briefing paper, or the full report at £9 plus 10 per cent p&p,

can be obtained from The Sainsbury Centre for Mental Health, 134–138 Borough High Street, London SE1 1LB.

(3) A local carers' group survey

This small, unpublished survey involved 21 out of a possible 22 families and they judged the following nine services to be a priority *at the time of a first episode* of a serious mental illness:

(i)   Support for the family

(ii)   Explanations about the illness

(iii) Explanations about the way that symptoms may affect the sufferer

(iv)   Explanations about the role of medication and any side effects

(v)   The potential risks of further breakdown

(vi)   The providing of a 'lifeline' – what to do if needing help in the future

(vii) Advice about the benefits system and other practical services

(viii) Introduction to self-help organizations and relevant literature

(ix)   Information for *the sufferer* about the illness and how to cope.

Over 80 per cent of the families received none of these perceived priorities *at the time of the first episode* of the sufferer's illness. Furthermore, 50 per cent had never received most of these services by the time they took part in the survey, despite further opportunities for this at times of relapse. Just one family received most of these services at the start of the sufferer's illness (Cooper, S. and Howe, G. (1993) reported in Howe, G. (1994) *Working with Schizophrenia*. London: Jessica Kingsley Publishers, pp.44–45, 73–76).

(4) Sharing information about the illness with the sufferer

Falloon and Talbot in their 1981 paper 'Achieving the goals of day treatment.' *Journal of Nervous and Mental Disease 170*, 5, 279–285, have described an educational programme they promoted in a hospital in the United States which provided regular seminars for recovering patients on matters such as diagnosis, possible causes and course of the illness and ways of coping with it. Emphasis was given to the role of medication, possible side effects and ways of dealing with these, and finding 'prompts for remembering to take medication at appropriate times'. Relatives were encouraged to join these sessions.

(5) A civil liberties issue or a duty to care and protect?

As we have noted, patients with a serious mental illness such as manic depression may lose their usual inhibitions and feel bound to spend their money recklessly and maybe to behave excessively out of character in other ways. When those who are meant to be caring for these patients pronounce that it is the patient's 'right' to behave however they wish – regardless of the consequences – they are denying their own duty to look after and protect their patients. As the latter are in hospital because they are having these sort of problems, we might wonder what role staff envisage for themselves if it is not to protect these patients from themselves?

EXERCISE

Do you feel that the recommendations which the LEAP group have made at the end of this chapter can be widely implemented? If you were commissioned to ensure that this was achieved, how would you go about it? Do you feel that these recommendations could contribute to a more positive outcome of a patient's serious mental illness and why? (or, why not? as the case may be).

CHAPTER 8

Hospital treatment and care
Summing up

In the previous chapters of this book we have looked at the sort of experiences which any one sufferer might have in hospital at any one time. We have looked at how the other victims of a serious mental illness have fared too – that is, those closest to the sufferer. In Chapters 2–6, the LEAP group has studied case studies of individual stays in hospital. In Chapter 7, members have gone on to consider in some detail their own experiences of hospital and those of their families and friends.

Let's now take a look at the group's findings while working on this book. Rather than making continual reference to one chapter or another, the names of the individuals concerned have been used and, if required, readers can find the relevant pages in the text under Case Studies in the Index. Some of the issues which have concerned members in *Hospital Treatment and Care* have also cropped up earlier in this series and we will deal with those first.

Delays in obtaining acknowledgement of a serious mental illness

As we have seen, Julie suffered these sorts of delays because the team supervising her interpreted her psychotic behaviour as the feigning of a psychotic illness. Meanwhile, she became increasingly ill and very much at risk. In *Getting into the System*, members found that younger new sufferers – particularly teenagers too young for the adult mental health services – were the ones most likely to suffer from lack of recognition of their illness. However, whatever the age of the sufferer, as we have seen, all the evidence points to a need for early intervention, which, of course, is known to be the rule rather than the exception with illnesses of all kinds.

Professionals declining to use the Mental Health Act

In *Getting into the System* and *Mental Health Assessments* the LEAP group found instances where professionals declined to use the law to protect a sufferer. This was certainly the case with Julie and the parents' pleas for her to be sectioned on several occasions were ignored by the GP and the hospital ward team despite all the available evidence that their daughter was desperately in need of help and protection. Meanwhile, she was allowed to do thousands of pounds damage to property and she and her family were given to understand it was their responsibility to pay for this damage and they did just that although members of the LEAP group would argue that the responsibility for this should be laid at the feet of those supervising the patient's treatment.

A lack of communication and explanations

This lack of communication and explanations for sufferers and families is an issue which has been raised several times in this book as well as earlier in the series. This phenomenon seems to be a feature which is evident from the very start of a serious mental illness – with no-one close to the sufferer knowing what is going on until there is a crisis and, probably, admission to hospital. In Chapter 7, we have quoted a survey which confirms this lack of communication and explanations but we have also seen quite startling examples of this in the case studies featuring Naomi and Joe and, once again, in Julie's unhappy story.

The undervaluing of families

At the end of *Getting into the System*, the LEAP group marvelled at the way families continue to be undervalued both as a source of information – for example, on the past history and on the day-to-day progress of a sufferer – but also as a major provider of community care. In the present book we find even more startling examples of families being under-valued – ignored even – with the worst example of this being Joe's case. Although this young man has been ill for several years and in hospital for much of that time, the family have still received no sensible communications from the psychiatrist and her team, nor any explanation for his illness.

In another two cases, husbands of sufferers have been virtually ignored by those supervising their wives' care; this happened to Naomi's husband, when he tried to find out what was the matter with his wife and whether or not she would ever be well enough to come out of hospital again and to Sue's husband, when hospital staff chose to believe her paranoid delusions about him even when it became clear that there was no evidence whatsoever to back these up. Furthermore, it seems that the rest of Sue's family and friends fared little better with this team.

Another family – Barry's – was virtually ignored during two of the years when he was severely ill and neglected by the system. When, at last, this young man was starting to become well again, his treatment was changed by a new psychiatrist and Barry's parents were once more excluded, this time by this doctor and the ward team. Yet it was his parents who had continued to 'stay in there' with him throughout this whole unhappy period and had provided continuity and sanctuary throughout the time the professionals allowed him to 'slip through the net'.

A connection between families being valued and patients doing well?

As we noted in Chapter 6, towards the end of the group's discussion on the dramatically different experiences of each of the sufferers featured, a survivor in the group pointed out that she felt that a pattern was emerging throughout this series which seemed to indicate that **patients flourished under the care of teams who acknowledged and valued their families too**. The group was intrigued by this seemingly valid comment and hopes that someone responsible for service provision, and looking for an interesting research subject, might be interested in further investigating this interesting observation!

A need for feedback

When working on the first two books in this series, the LEAP group found evidence, similar to their own experiences, which shows that professionals working on any one case rarely receive any feedback on the outcome. They can be involved in the crisis at any one point – albeit often briefly – and then hear nothing further about it. Instead of receiving feedback on the outcome of the case from their department they may hear nothing more, thus losing the opportunity to learn how their own decisions and input affected the patient's future well-being. LEAP members believe this is a major flaw in a system where a variety of theories and approaches are being used by those working with serious mental illness. It seemed to them at that time – and even more so later when working on the present book – that there is a marked lack of opportunity for individual workers to learn from their own experience what does and what doesn't work in the handling of a serious mental illness.

We have had ample evidence in the cases of Julie, Sue and Barry to demonstrate just how much this lack of feedback can be aggravated by a frequent lack of continuity in any one case. What, for example, are the chances of the first team which looked after Julie having learned anything from their experience with her? Are individual members of that team likely to learn that she is at last beginning to thrive and to pick up some of the threads of her previous life, following her stay in a specialist unit many miles away? Similarly, what are the chances that members of the ward team, who led Barry's parents to understand that he was suffering from the effects of poor family relationships rather than an illness, will have learned anything about his eventual, delayed, recovery – again miles away – out in the community, brought about when his former dose of medication was reinstated and maintained due to such good progress? Finally, what are the chances that individual members of the ward team which supervised Sue's care at the time of her second breakdown have learned anything from her speedy and dramatic transformation once the new medication started to work for her? One would imagine the chances are not very good, as not one of them chose to ask Sue about how it had been for her during those first wretched weeks on the ward and what sort of experiences had provoked her untypical behaviour during that time. Neither did anyone in the team later show any insight into Sue's pressing need to be able to talk about this with them, any more than they had recognized her need for care and attention when she was psychotic.

The sort of mistakes made in these cases were surely very serious ones and yet it seems likely that those involved in them will most probably have learned nothing further about serious mental illness as a result. How then, members of the group ask, can we hope for a general improvement and standardization of the services offered to its victims?

Professional training and expertise

This last point brings us to another factor which has been highlighted earlier in the series; members' concern about the lack of understanding and knowledge about psychosis amongst mental health professionals. They believe that this is becoming increasingly prevalent and that rivalry between the different disciplines has led to the adoption of a variety of approaches which in turn has contributed to an eroding of basic knowledge and expertise in the handling of serious mental illness. This situation has seemingly stemmed from a deliberate move away from the old medical hierarchy and the LEAP group feel that such considerations have led to a gradual rejection of a 'disease model' approach to psychotic illness. Members believe that things may be going badly wrong for the victims of a serious mental illness at the point where those supervising the case look for reasons other than illness to explain dramatic changes in the personality and behaviour of their patients.

Equally worrying, in the eyes of group, is the paradox whereby a sufferer can be in hospital – and by definition, therefore, a patient – and yet be denied the dignity of a sick role. To be in hospital and to be denied a reason for being there is demoralizing and confusing to say the least. Julie has described very clearly in Chapter 7 how this feels.

Some conclusions which merit further attention?

While working on *Hospital Treatment and Care*, members of the LEAP group have come up with several conclusions. These are detailed in the following sections.

A role for a nucleus of specially trained workers

While it seems likely that this adoption of various theories and approaches to psychosis will continue in the immediately foreseeable future anyway, members of the LEAP group have suggested consideration might be given to recruiting members of the different disciplines involved with this type of illness who would like to specialize in working with patients with this type of illness. There are already a few psychiatrists and other professionals who devote their time and energy to this unfashionable but major client population. A basic fund of knowledge and skills has been successfully developed over the past few decades which could be made available for training purposes, together with the very real expertise to be found among survivors and those closest to them who have found ways to successfully cope with a serious mental illness. The LEAP group members suggest that the building up of a group of specialist workers – from various disciplines – who could work with a limited caseload of individuals with severe mental illness should be encouraged and that these individuals should be available to assess patients where problems have arisen and to advise their colleagues as to the most appropriate approach in each case.

An urgent need for a right to an independent second opinion

The LEAP group is sure that while the approaches to a serious mental illness vary so dramatically, patients and/or their families should be able to seek a second opinion if they have no faith in the treatment being offered. This seems eminently reasonable when some doctors may delay in offering effective treatment for psychotic symptoms which are now known to be dangerous for these patients.

A role for a proper assessment

The LEAP group observed that Julie's predicament, when she was in the first hospital, demonstrated very clearly the need for a properly structured assessment process to be established. As we noted, one member who has worked in the mental health services asked 'Why did the hospital team decide her problem was "behavioural" without first exploring the possibility that she might be psychotic? Why look for deviance rather than illness? They knew she was depressed.' This protest was particularly relevant as members had discovered that Julie was not only a particularly intelligent young person; she was also apparently a well adjusted, active and productive student with a testimony from one of her tutors describing her as unusually mature, and courteous at all times. Members found her psychiatrist's comment a year or so later that she must learn to be responsible for her own destructive behaviour quite bizarre in these circumstances.

While working on the first two books in this series, members of the group pointed out the need for an agreed and structured assessment for every patient and that the starting point for this should be the building up of a clear picture of the patient's personality and lifestyle before things started going wrong. They believe that Julie's case is a particularly pertinent example of what can go wrong without this and how a proper diagnosis and appropriate treatment can be delayed indefinitely because of this. Finally, they were truly astonished by this case because it beggared belief that someone would wish to lay claim to a psychotic illness they didn't have. Julie's case had demonstrated quite clearly that those who believed in such a phenomenon had no way of differentiating between feigned psychosis and the real thing.

A role for an early diagnosis, treatment and explanations

It is perhaps not surprising that Julie stressed at the end of her testimony to the second psychiatrist and his team that she truly believed 'that the main factor in schizophrenia is diagnosis and early treatment'. Members of the group agree with this statement. Their own experiences, and that of many others, has long convinced them that this is the case; indeed, long before research began to confirm this reasonable viewpoint.

Members are equally convinced of the importance of sharing the diagnosis as soon as possible with the sufferer and family, with full explanations as to its implications. They insist, however, that it is crucial to get the timing of this right for the patient and that this should be done in a sensitive and positive way as soon as the he or she is starting to recover from a first episode of the illness. We have cited a paper describing one example of how this can be achieved in hospital, see (4) p.119.

A need for a standardization of services

Finally, the LEAP group concluded that the disturbing differences they have found in the treatment and care of any one individual on any one visit to hospital could only be put down to the varying theories and approaches being used by different professions and by different individuals within those professions. Furthermore, it seemed likely that any one ward team's approach was likely to be influenced by the most influential member of the team supervising the patient and this was not necessarily the psychiatrist. The group noted that there seemed to be just two main approaches in the seven ward teams described in the case studies in this book – quite simply, judgemental and non-judgemental – and that the former approach tended to be associated with teams which focused on patients' presenting behaviour at any one time rather than on their illness. Members were quite sure that these differences in approach should not be allowed to affect the standardization of one factor they considered to be of major importance to all patients with a serious mental illness, ie *the quality of care provided in hospital.*

Quality of care – some recommendations

After considering the experiences and comments of members of the LEAP group, their families and friends, in Chapter 7, the group came up with five basic needs of patients and those closest to them which they felt should be acknowledged and incorporated into the working policy of all hospital teams. As we noted, these needs were as follows:

(1) A need for respect; with particular emphasis on maintaining the dignity of patients.

(2) A need to be listened to; that anything the family or patient feel is important about the patient's psychiatric history, normal lifestyle, etc, should be carefully recorded and taken into account when decisions are being made.

(3) A need to know; that all information which can empower patients and their families to cope with the illness should be shared with them and that mediation should be made available if there is any conflict on confidentiality issues.

(4) A need to receive a proper welcome on admission to the ward; that patients and their families should be provided with written information on the ward's procedure and facilities and that a member of staff should extend a welcome and be available to answer any immediate queries they might have.

(5) A need for care and protection; that patients should be protected from the known risks of their illness and that civil rights issues should not be used as an excuse for not achieving this.

Members of the LEAP group feel that if these often unmet needs are acknowledged and incorporated into every ward team's policy, then such a move will go a long way to providing a standardized and desirable quality of care for psychiatric inpatients throughout England and Wales.

CONCLUSION

Once again, it bears saying that the LEAP group are not looking for, nor expecting, miracles. They do feel, however, that there is something very wrong when standards of care and treatment can vary as dramatically as we have demonstrated in this book. It is understandable that members of the group would like to see greater standardization in the services which patients receive. They hope that those responsible for the provision of this treatment and care in England and Wales are becoming aware of the startling anomalies which exist and that they will be receptive to any of the group's suggestions which indicate another way forward.

Glossary

The term serious (or severe) mental illness refers to those conditions which can cause sufferers to become psychotic, so losing touch with reality. The most common of these are schizophrenia and manic depression. The following brief, and inevitably over-simplified, definitions may help readers who are not well acquainted with these illnesses.

MANIC DEPRESSION (MD)

This illness is an 'affective' disorder with severe mood swings. The individual may at any one time experience profound depression or mania. Sufferers describe their depressive episodes as being enveloped by a dark cloud but many experience a manic episode as being exciting and euphoric; a brilliant and creative phase. That is, until their 'high' escalates out of control and they slip into a psychosis, at which point the euphoria can become a disaster, once more disrupting the sufferer's life.

Mania begins with a build-up of symptoms, including a general **speeding up of movement and speech; a lack of sleep; enhanced creativity and awareness; an inflated self-confidence**, alongside increasing **irritability and impatience with others**. There is often **pressure of speech** (a compulsive need to talk continuously); **flight of ideas** (an inability to follow through one line of thought or idea); **a disturbing loss of judgement** (putting the individual very much at risk); lots of grand ideas, including **preoccupation with spending money** and a **lack of inhibition** which, in some cases, can lead to uncharacteristic **promiscuity**. At this stage of a manic episode, it is not uncommon for the sufferer to experience some of the psychotic symptoms listed under 'acute' schizophrenia below.

The depressive episodes in MD may be seen as the 'down' and reverse side of mania, and the sufferer's experience may include a general **slowing down of movement and speech; a lack of energy and motivation; increased inhibition; impaired concentration and ability to undertake the simplest tasks; distorted feelings of**

guilt and self-loathing; anxiety and agitation and morbid thoughts of death, and worse, **suicidal ideas**. Severe depression can escalate into a psychosis with hallucinations and delusions, but this is not so common as with mania.

These days, the excess of MD can usually be controlled by one of the various mood-stabilizing drugs now available and the prognosis can be good. However, some individuals suffer distressing side-effects and one of these can be a dampening down of their often considerable creative ability which may make them reluctant to comply with treatment.

SCHIZOPHRENIA

The *acute* form of schizophrenia is characterized by a cluster of so-called 'positive' symptoms and these include (a) **hallucinations**, when any of, or all, five senses may play tricks on the individual, the most common being the 'hearing of voices', (b) **delusions**, when all sorts of incredible ideas become fixed beliefs in the individual's mind and impervious to any reasoned argument. The most distressing and damaging of these can be the **paranoia** which convinces sufferers that other people – usually those who matter most to them – are plotting against them and (c) **thought disturbance** with sufferers having all sorts of bizarre experiences such as finding their thoughts have taken on a life of their own, leading to ideas that their minds have been taken over by an outside source. These then are examples of the sort of experiences we call 'positive' symptoms, which make up the main part of an 'acute' schizophrenic illness. They are usually controlled by anti-psychotic medication but some 'acute' sufferers relapse into further psychotic episodes, particularly if they cut down or discontinue their medication. Because of this, there is an urgent need for a preventive approach to the handling of this illness.

The *chronic* form of schizophrenia is characterized by an ongoing and persistent cluster of 'negative' symptoms (so called because they take something away from the individual's original personality) which are disabling and in many ways quite different to those of acute schizophrenia. These include severe **lethargy**; profound **apathy**; **poverty of speech**, precluding any real ability to initiate conversation or indulge in what we know as 'small talk', **impaired concentration**, making it difficult to even read a few lines of a newspaper; **emotional**

blunting, in which sufferers may demonstrate no interest in or emotions about those closest to them and a general flatness in a 'grey' world where they feel no anticipation or excitement, with none of the highs and lows most of us experience in everyday life. All this can be socially crippling and amount to severe impairment and a change in personality which can make sufferers, and those closest to them, feel they have lost the person they once knew.

Despite the differences in the 'acute' and 'chronic' forms of the illness, there is an overlap between them. 'Acute' sufferers can experience some of these 'negative' symptoms following a breakdown and, tragically, some slip into the chronic form of the illness after one breakdown too many. Similarly, many 'chronic' sufferers can relapse into acute episodes of the illness, particularly if they are not protected by 'maintenance' medication.

General Glossary

Advance Directive: a device by which sufferers can make a declaration, when well, about what they would want to happen if they become ill again. There is growing interest in using this tool as a kind of insurance against becoming entirely dependent upon a bureaucratic system to make important decisions which can affect the rest of the individual's life.

Anti-psychotic medication: see Neuroleptic Medication.

Approved Social Worker (ASW): a professional, without medical training, who is qualified to work with the mental health law and to determine whether or not to make application for a sufferer's compulsory admission to hospital (given the required medical recommendations are available).

Community Psychiatric Nurse (CPN): a professional who provides ongoing support and care for the patient in the community. Also monitors medication and gives injections.

Critical Period: the limited time before a breakdown when sufferers realize they are relapsing and in need of help.

Delusion: a firmly held belief which has no basis in reality.

Depot Injection: an injection into the muscle tissue of neuroleptic medication which is then slowly released, lasting anything from one to four weeks.

Family Theories: popular theories from the 1960s and 1970s, now discredited, which blamed families for their relative's schizophrenic illness.

Genetic Risk: while we all have a one per cent chance of becoming schizophrenic at some time during our lives, research points to a raised risk in individuals with relatives who are sufferers; with one parent or brother or sister – 10 per cent, with two parents – 30 per cent, with an identical twin – 45 per cent.

GP: a doctor providing general medical treatment and care within the community who is the 'gateway' to all psychiatric services. Can also recommend their patient's compulsory admission to hospital.

Hallucination: an altered or abnormal perception affecting one's hearing, vision, taste, smell or touch. The most common type is auditory – the 'hearing of voices' for which there is no rational explanation.

Labelling Theory: popular theory originating from the 1960s claiming that a diagnosis of mental illness is little more than a stigmatized label put on someone who is 'deviant'. Consequently, professionals (rather than sufferers and their families) still tend to avoid acknowledging psychotic illness.

Mental Health Assessment: an assessment to determine whether or not someone mentally ill needs to be compulsorily admitted to hospital.

Nearest Relative: Defined by the law and often the elder of a sufferer's parents or the spouse. Has certain rights, including that of making application for the individual's compulsory admission to hospital (given the required medical recommendations are available) if an ASW declines to do this.

Neuroleptic Medication: the drugs which have been used since the early 1950s to control psychotic symptoms. Also known as anti-psychotic drugs. New ones have become available during the 1990s, helping some of those unaffected by the original medication.

Occupational Therapist: a professional who works with individuals or groups of patients in hospital or in the community, facilitating rehabilitation and supporting them in adapting to an appropriate lifestyle.

Paranoia: possibly the most damaging and disruptive of all the delusional symptoms of a psychotic illness. This manifests itself particularly at times of breakdown and typically involves those who matter most to the patient; very often close family.

Personality Disorder: a little understood blanket term and an unwelcome label received by many individuals with a serious mental illness before their psychotic behaviour is properly understood and diagnosed.

Police: often involved in crisis work; can use the Mental Health Act, 1983, to take someone from a public area to a 'safe place' such as hospital or police station if they appear to be seriously mentally ill, so that a Mental Health Assessment can be arranged.

Psychiatric Nurse: a professional who can work within a hospital, a formal hostel or the community, providing nursing care and support and the monitoring and administration of medication. See also CPN.

Psychiatrist: a specialist doctor in charge of patients' psychiatric treatment in hospital and in the community. Can also recommend, when appropriate, any individual for compulsory admission to hospital.

Psychosis: a condition in which sufferers lose touch with reality and have no recognition of the fact that they are mentally ill and in need of help. When this happens, it usually means that treatment cannot be administered unless professionals use the mental health law to admit the individual to hospital.

Sectioning: the use of the law to compulsorily admit someone with a mental illness to hospital.

Serious Mental Illness: this is the name we give to conditions such as manic depression and schizophrenia which can cause the individual to sometimes lose touch with reality, ie, to become psychotic.

Social Worker: a professional concerned with arranging accommodation for patients and assessing, as appropriate, other practical needs. May provide support for sufferers in the community and/or their families, usually on a short-term basis. An approved social worker (ASW) may set up a mental health assessment and go on to apply for the individual's compulsory admission under the Mental Health Act.

Further Reading

Copeland, M.E. (1994) *Living with Depression and Manic Depression.* Harbinger Publications Incorporated.

Beautifully presented and useful book from the USA by an MD sufferer and campaigner. She outlines a day-by-day self-management approach to coping with this type of illness (which could perhaps best be described as 'working in partnership' with professionals and a selected group of supporters). Includes advice on drawing up advance directives, and generally brings a new meaning to the words 'self-determination'.

Department of Health and Welsh Office (1993) *Code of Practice: Mental Health Act 1983.* London: HMSO. Available from HMSO, PO Box 276, London SW8 5DT (Tel: 0171 873 9090).

The *Code of Practice* should really be mandatory reading for all professionals who work with the seriously mentally ill or, at the very least, be made readily available for everyone at the work place. Also useful for families caught up in a crisis situation which may call for resort to the law.

Howe, G. (1991) *The Reality of Schizophrenia.* London: Faber & Faber.

By the present author, this book sets out to explain the historical perspective and content of all the 'muddled thinking', as she puts it, surrounding schizophrenia.

Howe, G. (1995) *Working with Schizophrenia: A Needs Based Approach.* London: Jessica Kingsley Publishers.

This book was written by the present author, with contributions from sufferers and carers and several professional colleagues. Primarily written for individuals working with this illness, it has been warmly received by the relevant professional journals as well as by organizations involved with sufferers and carers.

Howe, G. (1997) *Serious Mental Illness: A Family Affair.* London: Sheldon Press.

This book, by the present author, is written to help lay-people understand conditions such as manic depression and schizophrenia. In particular, it is for sufferers and families trying to cope with this type of illness. It covers practical issues such as getting the best from the system, coping in a crisis and, perhaps more important, how to avoid a crisis!

Kuipers, L. and Bebbington, P. (2nd edition, 1997) *Living With Mental Illness.* London: Souvenir Press Ltd (Human Horizon Series).

Written by a psychologist and psychiatrist for relatives of the mentally ill; families should find this eminently readable book informative and helpful.

Manic Depression Fellowship (1995) *Inside Out: A Guide to Self Management of Manic Depression.* Produced and published by Manic Depression Fellowship (see under Useful Addresses).

This innovative and valuable booklet reflects the enthusiasm among the membership of MDF for a self-management approach to coping with this illness.

Manic Depression Fellowship (1997) *A Balancing Act.* Produced and published by Manic Depression Fellowship (see under Useful Addresses).

An extremely useful book. To quote MDF's *Pendulum*, 'It is aimed at the people who live alongside and help those who have a diagnosis of MD. It includes techniques and strategies which carers have found helpful.'

Varma, V. (1997) *Managing Manic Depressive Disorders.* London: Jessica Kingsley Publishers.

Provides useful information and analysis for people who are concerned with manic depressives. Discusses the possibilities of treatment and self-management.

Useful Addresses

Depression Alliance
35 Westminster Bridge Road
London SE1 7JB
Tel: 0171 633 0557
Concerned with helping sufferers and their families to cope with a depressive illness. Provides advice and information about the illness and seeks to educate public opinion. Quarterly newsletter, *A Single Step*.

Making Space
46 Allen Street
Warrington
Cheshire WA2 7JB
Tel: 01925 571680
As well as offering advice and support for a membership of nearly three thousand families who have to cope with a serious mental illness, Making Space provides a wide range of community facilities across the North West of England and Yorkshire and employs a team of Family Support Workers to help carers and sufferers.

Manic Depression Fellowship (MDF)
8–10 High Street
Kingston-upon-Thames
Surrey KT1 1EY
Tel: 0181 974 6550
Offers information, advice and support to those having to cope with MD, frequent open meetings and local self-help groups. Also involved in campaigning for better services. Quarterly journal, *Pendulum*, which includes a regular summary of relevant research.

National Schizophrenia Fellowship (NSF)
18 Castle Street
Kingston-upon-Thames
Surrey KT1 1SS
Tel: 0181 547 3937
Concerned with helping those affected by serious mental illness, while providing community services and promoting education and knowledge. Conferences and training days and local self-help groups throughout England

and Wales. Quarterly newsletter, *NSF Today*. Highly recommended helpline: 0181 974 6814 (10am–3pm weekdays).

SANE
Cityside House
40 Adler Street
London E1 1EE
Tel: 0171 375 1002
Concerned with research, campaigning and promoting knowledge about serious mental illness. Pioneering research at SANE's Prince of Wales International Centre in Oxford. Occasional newsletter, *Sanetalk*. SANE Helpline: 0171 724 8000 (afternoons, evenings and weekends).

Schizophrenia Association of Great Britain (SAGB)
International Schizophrenia Centre
Bryn Hyfryd
The Crescent
Bangor
Gwynedd LL57 2AG
Tel: 01248 354048
Involved in biochemical research into schizophrenia and helping sufferers and families to cope with the illness. Occasional newsletter.

The Sainsbury Centre for Mental Health
134–138 Borough High Street
London SE1 1LB
Tel: 0171 403 8790
The Centre is concerned with *Working for Excellence in Mental Health Services* and provides conferences and publications as well as carrying out research to this end.

Subject
Index

Name Index